D0871009

WITHDRAWN
FROM THE RECORDS OF THE
MID-CONTINENT PUBLIC LIBRARY

636.6803 AL23 2003
Alderton, David
Illustrated encyclopedia of
  caged & aviary birds

MID-CONTINENT PUBLIC LIBRARY
Grandview Branch
12930 Booth Lane
Grandview, MO 64030 **GV**

ILLUSTRATED ENCYCLOPEDIA OF

CAGED & AVIARY
BIRDS

ILLUSTRATED ENCYCLOPEDIA OF

CAGED & AVIARY
BIRDS

*A comprehensive visual guide to pet
birds of the world*

DAVID ALDERTON

LORENZ BOOKS

MID-CONTINENT PUBLIC LIBRARY
Grandview Branch
12930 Booth Lane
Grandview, MO 64030
GV

MID-CONTINENT PUBLIC LIBRARY

3 0000 12517652 3

This edition is published by Lorenz Books

Lorenz Books is an imprint of Anness Publishing Ltd
Hermes House, 88–89 Blackfriars Road, London SE1 8HA
tel. 020 7401 2077; fax 020 7633 9499
www.lorenzbooks.com; info@anness.com

© Anness Publishing Ltd 1996, 2003

UK agent: The Manning Partnership Ltd,
6 The Old Dairy, Melcombe Road, Bath BA2 3LR;
tel. 01225 478 444; fax 01225 478 440; sales@manning-partnership.co.uk

UK distributor: Grantham Book Services Ltd,
Isaac Newton Way, Alma Park Industrial Estate, Grantham, Lincs NG31 9SD;
tel. 01476 541080; fax 01476 541061; orders@gbs.tbs-ltd.co.uk

North American agent/distributor: National Book Network,
4501 Forbes Boulevard, Suite 200, Lanham, MD 20706;
tel. 301 459 3366; fax 301 429 5746; www.nbnbooks.com

Australian agent/distributor: Pan Macmillan Australia,
Level 18, St Martins Tower, 31 Market St, Sydney, NSW 2000;
tel. 1300 135 113; fax 1300 135 103; customer.service@macmillan.com.au

All rights reserved. No part of this publication may be reproduced, stored in a retrieval system,
or transmitted in any way or by any means, electronic, mechanical, photocopying, recording or
otherwise, without the prior written permission of the copyright holder.

A CIP catalogue record for this book is available from the British Library.

Publisher Joanna Lorenz
Managing Editor Judith Simons
Project Editor Sarah Ainley
Designer Michael Morey
Jacket Design White Light
Indexer Helen Snaith
Production Controller Yolande Denny

Previously published as *The Encyclopedia of Caged and Aviary Birds*

1 3 5 7 9 10 8 6 4 2

PICTURE CREDITS

t=top; b=bottom; c=centre; l=left; r=right

Dennis Avon 1; 2; 3; 5, 6bl; 8; 10; 11t; 11b; 12tr; 12b; 13t; 13b; 14t; 14b; 16t; 17t; 17b; 18t; 18b; 19b; 20t; 21t; 21c; 21b; 22; 25t; 25c; 27br; 28t; 28b; 29t; 29c; 29b; 30tl; 30tr; 30b; 31t; 31c; 31b; 32tl; 32c; 32b; 33t; 33bl; 33br; 34; 36; 37t; 37b; 38; 39b; 42; 43t; 43b; 44t; 44b; 46t; 49b; 51; 52c; 53b; 56tr; 56bl; 57t; 57b; 58tl; 58bl; 58br; 59tl; 59tr; 59br; 61br; 62cl; 62br; 83bl; 64t; 65t; 66b; 67t; 67cl; 68tl; 69t; 69b; 70b; 71t; 71b; 73b; 74t; 74b; 75cl; 78bc; 79tr; 79cr; 79br; 82t; 82c; 86; 87t; 87c; 87b; 88t; 88c; 88b; 89t; 89b; 90; 92; 93t; 93b; 95tr; 95bl; 96t; 96b; 97b; 99t; 99b; 101t; 102; 103t; 103b; 105t; 105b; 108; 109t; 114t; 115b; 118t; 118b; 119br; 123b; 126; 129b. **John Daniels** 6t; 7t. **Cyril Laubscher** 7b; 12tl; 15t; 15c; 15b; 16b; 19t; 20b; 25t; 26; 35; 39t; 40; 41; 45t; 45b; 46b; 47; 48b; 49t; 50t; 50b; 52br; 53t; 54; 60t; 60bl; 60br; 61t; 61bl; 62t; 62c; 63t; 63br; 64bl; 64br; 65b; 67b; 68tr; 68bc; 68br; 70t; 72t; 72b; 75t; 75b; 76; 77; 78bl; 79tl; 80; 81; 82b; 83t; 83b; 84; 94bl; 94br; 95tl; 95br; 97t; 98; 100; 101b; 104; 106; 107t; 107b; 109b; 110; 111t; 111b; 112; 113r; 114b; 115t; 116; 118c; 119t; 119c; 120; 121t; 121b; 122; 123t; 125t; 125b; 127t. **Tony Tilford** 23; 24b; 25bl; 48t; 58tr; 73t; 113l; 124.

CONTENTS

INTRODUCTION

Birds have been popular as pets for at least 4,000 years, dating back to the time of the ancient Egyptians. Today, their appeal as companions spans the globe. The talking abilities of parrots, for instance, enchant owners living in stylish apartments in Paris, New York or London as much as tribespeople living in scattered village communities across the Amazon basin or in the rainforests of West Africa. When European settlers arrived in Australia in the 1700s they started to keep one of the smaller native parakeets as pets. Since then, these birds, better known as budgerigars, have become the most widely kept birds in the world.

✦ RIGHT
The Gouldian finch is one of the world's most colourful finches, and this is one of the reasons why it is so popular. A number of different colour varieties have now been created.

✦ ABOVE
Budgerigars, a form of Australian parakeet, are known for their friendly temperament, as well as for their powers of mimicry. These birds are not demanding to keep, but if they are housed outdoors they must have a dry and well-lit shelter.

It is not just their powers of mimicry, however, that have attracted people to keeping birds as pets; the song of the canary was responsible for the introduction of these rather plain-coloured, greenish finches to Europe in the late 1400s, from the Canary Islands off the west coast of Africa. Now, domestic canaries possess singing abilities that are vastly superior to those of their wild relatives. Canaries have also evolved into birds displaying a wide range of colours; many distinctive varieties have been developed, which are popular for exhibition purposes. The exotic appearance and coloration of softbills and finches underlies their popularity. They are a constant source of fascination in a suitable aviary, and the challenge of breeding such birds successfully appeals to many people. The same applies to pheasants and doves, and these will thrive particularly well in a planted aviary.

Caring for birds has become much more straightforward over recent years, thanks to a better understanding of their nutritional needs. Special foods for all types of birds, ranging from hummingbirds to flamingos, are produced

◆ BELOW
This buff-feathered hen is a good example of the Norwich canary. Note the typically stocky body shape.

◆ RIGHT
This green-naped lorikeet would be well suited to aviary accommodation as part of a colony. Bear in mind that these birds can be very noisy.

commercially, with each one formulated to match particular needs. This, in turn, has been valuable in persuading pairs to breed successfully. Better general health means that if a bird does fall ill there is a greater chance of recovery. Advances in the field of equipment have helped to revolutionize the housing of birds, which contributes to their overall well-being.

Many people start out with a single pet bird and before long decide to construct an aviary. The exhibition side of the hobby often appeals to people once they have experience of bird breeding. Local clubs, catering for all types of birds, usually stage an annual show, and these provide an ideal way to meet fellow enthusiasts in your area, even if you are not interested in exhibiting. National groups cater for particular types of birds, such as parrots or budgerigars, and the larger ones may operate through local branches. They usually produce an annual newsletter or magazine for their members, keeping them up-to-date with the latest information and details of shows. You can track down information about local or national bird clubs through bird-keeping publications, libraries or via the Internet.

◆ BELOW
This pair of blue dacnis should be housed with birds of a similar size. They are not hardy birds, and will require heated winter accommodation.

WAXBILLS AND RELATED SPECIES

This family of finches is widely distributed across Africa, Asia and Australia. Many species are popular avicultural subjects, to the extent of being fully domesticated in some cases, such as the zebra finch. From a bird-keeping standpoint, they can be broadly divided into three categories. There are the African waxbills, so called because the red colour of their bills resembles sealing wax. The second category consists of the nuns or mannikins, found mainly in Asia and also in parts of north Africa. Their plumage is relatively subdued, comprising various shades of brown, black and cream. Finally, there are the Australian grassfinches, which are widely distributed across that continent.

♦ OPPOSITE

The Gouldian finch is one of the most colourful finches in the world, as well as one of the most commonly-kept in bird-keeping circles.

♦ LEFT

Lively and active by nature, this star finch is a typical example of its group. Such birds show to best effect in aviary surroundings, rather than in cages.

WAXBILLS

These small finches, averaging 10–13 cm (4–5 in) long, have been popular with both novice and experienced bird-keepers for many years. Waxbills make delightful occupants of a planted aviary in mixed- or single-species groups, although housing the birds in flocks of single species provides the greatest chance of breeding success. Blue waxbills are best housed in single pairs, unless the aviary is particularly large, because the cock bird of the dominant pair is likely to bully similarly coloured birds, especially during the breeding season.

BLUE WAXBILLS

There are three different species of blue waxbill, all of which are represented in aviculture. The most colourful, and also the easiest to sex, is the red-cheeked cordon bleu (*Uraeginthus bengalus*), so called because of the distinctive red cheek patches of the cock bird. In common with other members of the group, its underparts are an attractive sky-blue colour, offset against light brown upperparts. Hens are paler in colour, and they also lack the red areas on the sides of the head. A rare colour change has been recorded in some cock birds of this species; they have yellowish-orange rather than red cheek patches. The red-cheeked cordon bleu inhabits northern parts of Africa.

In the blue-capped cordon bleu (*U. cyanocephala*), the blue plumage is more extensive and covers the entire head of the cock bird. Hens show some brown feathering on the top of their heads, with brown present on the centre of the abdomen. This species is found in north-eastern Africa.

The third member of the genus is known as the cordon bleu or the blue-breasted cordon bleu (*U. angolensis*). It has grey plumage on the abdomen, with hens being paler than cocks in colour. The cordon bleu originates from southern parts of Africa.

All three blue waxbills require careful acclimatization before they can be allowed access to an aviary in temperate areas. Do not allow them

outside until all risk of frost has passed, and preferably when the weather is more settled. Problems are most likely to arise at this stage if the birds cannot find easy access to food, so it is worthwhile confining them beforehand in the aviary shelter, where food and water should be located.

Blue waxbills require a foreign finch seed mixture that contains various millets and other small seeds such as niger. They also feed readily on fresh grass seeds, chickweed and millet sprays. Livefoods such as micro-crickets are vital for the rearing of chicks. The birds seek out insects at this stage and the chicks will be neglected if these are not available.

Heated accommodation is essential for the blue waxbills during the cold, dark winter months, with artificial lighting to increase the length of the feeding period. A large flight cage will serve the purpose, but an indoor flight will provide the birds with more space and can help to keep them fitter.

BREED BOX	
Length	13 cm (5 in)
Incubation period	12 days
Fledging period	21 days
Clutch size	3–6 eggs

◆ BELOW
Waxbills such as this attractive pair of red-cheeked cordon bleus require careful management at first, but may then live for a decade or more.

RED-EARED WAXBILLS

◆ BELOW
Red-eared waxbills are hard to sex outside the
breeding season. Two birds preening each other
does not signify they are a pair, because they are
social birds by nature.

The majority of waxbills have more brown feathering in their plumage than the blues, such as the red-eared waxbill (*Estrilda troglodytes*) which occurs in northern Africa, south of the Sahara. Sexing can be difficult outside the breeding season, when the underparts of cock birds become a more colourful shade of pink. The red patches on the sides of the head are not helpful because of a similar species, the St Helena waxbill (*E. astrild*), which has almost identical facial markings, although the brown barring on its body is more prominent. The most obvious difference is that the red-eared waxbill has a blackish rump, extending over the surface of its tail feathers.

Breeding results are usually better if a group of red-eared waxbills are housed together, so if you make a mistake when picking out pairs, this is not necessarily significant. As the breeding season approaches, the cock bird displays to his intended mate, holding a blade of nesting material in his bill. Pairs usually prefer to construct their own nests, although they may occasionally use a covered nesting basket. The nest is woven using grass stems, coconut fibre and similar material, and is quite bulky. There is an obvious opening on the top, leading into a chamber that remains empty, with a concealed entrance into another chamber below. The first chamber is referred to as the cock's nest, and is designed to distract any predators, who will find the nest apparently empty.

BREED BOX

Length	10 cm (4 in)
Incubation period	12 days
Fledging period	21 days
Clutch size	4–5 eggs

ORANGE-CHEEKED WAXBILLS

A species with very similar requirements to the red-eared waxbill is the attractive orange-cheeked waxbill (*E. melpoda*). Relatively long, straggly claws help these birds to maintain a grip on thin branches in the wild, where they inhabit reedy areas, but within the confines of the aviary they can be hazardous. It is, therefore, important to clip the claws back before the start of the breeding season, so that the birds do not become caught up in their quarters.

The broad orange cheek patches enable this species to be identified without difficulty, but recognizing true pairs on the basis of differences in their plumage is very difficult. Hens may have paler coloration overall, but this is not entirely reliable. The display of the cock bird provides the best way of distinguishing between the sexes. He swaggers along the perch, swinging his tail from side to side, with a piece of nesting material in his bill; he also sings quite loudly. Seclusion is very important for breeding success because these waxbills can be nervous when nesting.

BREED BOX

Length	10 cm (4 in)
Incubation period	12 days
Fledging period	21 days
Clutch size	4–6 eggs

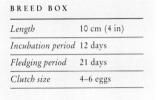

◆ BELOW
The characteristic orange feathering on the cheeks of these waxbills starts to develop from the age of about six weeks.

LAVENDER FINCHES

◆ BELOW
Lavender finches often become
quite tame in aviary surroundings.
They are agile birds, clambering up
and down branches like tits.

The lavender finch (*E. caerulescens*) is less colourful than some waxbills but it is still very attractive, with a bluish-grey body, offset against the red of the rump and the tail feathers. Hens can often be difficult to distinguish but may be paler.

Lavender finches generally agree well in groups, but they may show a tendency to pluck each other's feathers if housed in cages. When transferred to a flight or aviary, their plumage soon grows again. Pairs nest reliably in a well-planted aviary, particularly if provided with a box bush (*Buxus*).

A closely related variety, the black-tailed lavender finch (*E. perreini*), is distinguishable by the colour of its tail feathers, which are black in colour, rather than reddish.

◆ LEFT
Black-tailed lavender finches are not often seen in collections. They should be looked after in the same way as the lavender finch. Note the black bill and tail.

BREED BOX	
Length	10 cm (4 in)
Incubation period	12 days
Fledging period	19 days
Clutch size	3–5 eggs

FIREFINCHES

Firefinches are so-called because the cock birds are predominantly red. The hens are mainly brown, so sexing is quite straightforward. The red-billed firefinch (*Lagonosticta senegala*) is probably the most widely kept of its group. Firefinches need very careful management at first, and it is essential that they have heated winter-time accommodation. Pairs breed readily. Arrange the aviary so that the plants are under cover, because this lessens the risk of a nest site being chosen that may later be flooded. It also helps if the flight itself is enclosed on one side with tongue-and-groove timber, to give these small birds protection against wind and rain.

BREED BOX	
Length	10 cm (4 in)
Incubation period	12 days
Fledging period	19 days
Clutch size	3–5 eggs

◆ RIGHT
A cock red-billed firefinch displays its unmistakable colour. Chicks of both sexes are a similar shade of greyish-brown at first.

GOLDEN-BREASTED WAXBILLS

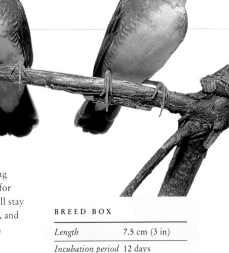

Another colourful waxbill that ranges over much of Africa to the south of the Sahara is the golden-breasted waxbill (*Amandava subflava*). It is the smallest member of the group, averaging about 7.5 cm (3 in) in size. The underparts are orangey-yellow in colour. They have a reddish eye stripe and brownish wings, with barring running down the sides of the body. Hens lack the eye stripe and are a duller shade.

Golden-breasted waxbills are one of the most adaptable members of the genus, to the extent of nesting in finch nesting baskets or boxes in breeding cages. Nesting material should be provided to enable the birds to line their nests. In view of the small size of these waxbills, cage fronts must be of a foreign finch design with suitably narrow bar spacing.

Both adult birds share the task of caring for the chicks, which should start to hatch after an incubation period of approximately 12 days. Small livefoods, including whiteworm and aphids, are vital for rearing the chicks. The young will stay in the nest for up to three weeks, and will continue to return here for a period after they have fledged.

◆ ABOVE RIGHT
This pair of golden-breasted waxbills shows the brighter colours of the cock bird. Note also that only the cock bird has the red eye stripe.

BREED BOX

Length	7.5 cm (3 in)
Incubation period	12 days
Fledging period	21 days
Clutch size	4–6 eggs

CUT-THROAT FINCHES

The cut-throat finch (*Amadina fasciata*) is one of the largest members of the group at approximately 12.5 cm (5 in) long. This species is instantly recognizable by the bright red patch across the throat of the cock bird.

Cut-throats are not generally recommended as companions for smaller waxbills because they tend to be aggressive, particularly when breeding. They can be housed in groups of the same species, on their own or with other birds of similar size such as Java sparrows.

Breeding is relatively straightforward, particularly as pairs can often be persuaded to use nest boxes, which they will line with nesting material. Do not provide nesting sites while the weather is still cold because hen cut-throats are vulnerable to egg-binding, which can arise as a result of chilling. It is vital to provide cuttlefish bone or a calcium supplement to ensure the eggshells are properly formed. In addition to livefood, cut-throats may also be persuaded to take a proprietary egg food, which should be supplied fresh each day.

BREED BOX

Length	12.5 cm (5 in)
Incubation period	12 days
Fledging period	21 days
Clutch size	3–5 eggs

◆ LEFT
The characteristic red throat marking that distinguishes the male cut-throat is very dramatic. The depth of the brown colour elsewhere on the body, and the markings themselves, may vary between individuals.

◆ LEFT
The cock bird of this pair of red avadavats is more darkly coloured than the hen. These birds construct a large domed nest in vegetation, often quite close to the ground.

RED AVADAVATS

The red avadavat or tiger finch (*Amandava amandava*) has a wide range across southern Asia, from India to parts of China and Indonesia. It is easy to tell when these birds are coming into breeding condition because this is when cock birds develop their rich red feathering, offset against dark brown wings. Those originating from the eastern part of the species range are sometimes called strawberry finches, and are recognizable by their brighter red underparts and small white spots on the wings. Hens are duller in colour but pairs are similar in appearance outside the breeding season. These birds may develop black patches of plumage. This is known as acquired melanism. It will disappear when the birds are transferred to more spacious surroundings and are given a more varied diet.

BREED BOX	
Length	10 cm (4 in)
Incubation period	12 days
Fledging period	19 days
Clutch size	4–6 eggs

NUNS

These relatives of the waxbills are found in Africa and Asia. They are highly social by nature, and good breeding results are most likely if the birds are kept in flocks comprising a single species. The birds' claws grow quickly, and may need to be clipped back to prevent the birds from becoming caught up in their aviary surroundings.

◆ LEFT
Pairs of African silverbills generally nest readily. They are not dependent on livefood for rearing their chicks.

SILVERBILLS

The silverbill (*Lonchura malabarica*) is one of the most widely distributed species of nun, ranging from northern parts of Africa across Asia as far as the Indian subcontinent. Like other members of this group, silverbills' plumage is predominantly brown; the Asian form is distinguished from its African relative by its black rump. It is impossible to sex these finches visually, but cocks can be recognized by their song. They are very easy birds to cater for, living well in groups. Pairs nest readily, often using a finch nesting basket or nesting box. Indian silverbills are especially prolific, laying clutches of up to 10 eggs and rearing two broods of chicks in a season. Pairs nest quite successfully in breeding cages, feeding on a mixture of millets and similar seeds. Egg food is usually taken when there are young in the nest, helping to raise the protein level of the birds' diet.

BREED BOX	
Length	10 cm (4 in)
Incubation period	12 days
Fledging period	21 days
Clutch size	4–8 eggs

BENGALESE OR SOCIETY FINCHES

The most widely kept member of this group is a bird that does not occur in the wild. The Bengalese, better known in North America as the society finch (*L. domestica*), is thought to be a fertile hybrid, developed from pairings of the striated munia (*L. striata acuticauda*) in China more than 300 years ago. A number of different colour mutations are established, including chocolate, fawn, pied and crested forms.

Bengalese are popular exhibition birds, usually being shown in matched pairs rather than as individuals. They are highly valued as foster parents in view of their steady natures, and are used to rear Gouldian finches, among others.

Visual sexing is impossible, so the only straightforward means of recognizing pairs is by the song of cock birds. It is

◆ LEFT
The self chocolate variety of the Bengalese or society finch, as seen here, is closest to the ancestral form of this domesticated finch.

◆ RIGHT
This is the fawn mutation of the Bengalese. These birds are called society finches in North America because of their sociable natures.

useful to band birds that you know are cocks. Celluloid rings that clip around the leg are invaluable for this purpose; they can be fitted at any age and are produced in a range of colours so you can distinguish individuals easily. In spite of their small size, Bengalese may live for seven years or more. These finches are highly recommended if you are keen to keep small birds in the home, with pairs often breeding well in suitable cages.

◆ LEFT
This is a chestnut and white Bengalese finch. The markings of these pied birds are variable; pairing two matching individuals is not necessarily a guarantee that their offspring will be similarly marked.

BREED BOX

Length	13 cm (5 in)
Incubation period	12 days
Fledging period	21 days
Clutch size	5–6 eggs

TRI-COLOURED NUNS

The tri-coloured nun (*L. malacca*) ranges eastwards across Asia to the Philippines and Indonesia. It is a popular species, invariably looking very sleek, and agreeing well with other birds as part of a mixed collection. Because of the problem in sexing these birds visually, starting out with a small group offers the best hope of obtaining at least one true pair. The birds' claws often become straggly, and need to be carefully trimmed back prior to releasing them into an outdoor aviary.

Once acclimatized, these birds are relatively hardy, but they still need a sheltered aviary and heated accommodation if the winter is harsh. Good breeding results are most likely to be obtained in a planted flight with stands of bamboo of suitable size helping to provide a secure nesting environment for them. The hens lay between three and five eggs, with incubation lasting 12–13 days. The young fledge when they are about three weeks old. Livefood plays very little part in the diet of these birds when they have chicks, so it is often easier to rear them than waxbills.

BREED BOX

Length	10 cm (4 in)
Incubation period	13 days
Fledging period	20 days
Clutch size	3–5 eggs

◆ ABOVE
The combination of cream, black and chestnut-brown plumage marks out the tri-coloured nun. These finches are reasonably hardy once acclimatized.

MAGPIE MANNIKINS

The magpie mannikin (*L. fringilloides*) is one of the best known of the African mannikins in bird-keeping circles. Its requirements are identical to the tri-coloured nun's. Pairs of magpie mannikins can be aggressive when ready to nest and, in view of

◆ RIGHT
The magpie or pied mannikin is found in Africa rather than Asia. The name comes from the fact that its plumage is predominantly black and white.

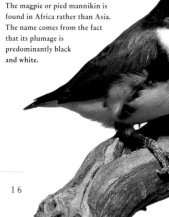

their powerful bills, it is better to keep them on their own rather than mix them with waxbills. It is also not a good idea to keep individual mannikins of different species together because they may pair up and produce unwanted hybrid offspring. If they are to be kept in a group on their own, take care that the birds are not overcrowded, as this can greatly reduce the likelihood that they will breed successfully. Although magpie mannikins are so-called because of their predominantly black

BREED BOX

Length	13 cm (5 in)
Incubation period	12 days
Fledging period	21 days
Clutch size	4–6 eggs

and white plumage, resembling a magpie, young birds of this species are much browner in colour when they first leave the nest. It will take several months for them to moult into adult plumage, after which they will be indistinguishable from their parents, unless they have been ringed. Band the young birds with split rings soon after fledging for this reason.

JAVA SPARROWS

◆ ABOVE
The Java sparrow originates from south-eastern Asia. Visual sexing is difficult, although cocks may sometimes be picked out by their larger bills. Their song provides a more reliable indicator of their gender.

The Java sparrow or rice bird (*Padda oryzivora*) is the largest member of the group, averaging about 15cm (6in) long. The white form has been kept in the Orient for centuries, but other colour forms have been developed over recent years. The most common is an attractive fawn variety, and there are greys and fawn pieds. Cock birds have a very pleasant song.

Java sparrows should be mixed only with companions of similar size such as weavers, or possibly cockatiels, if not being kept in a group or on their own. Often only the dominant pair will breed, but the presence of others of their kind seems to encourage breeding activity.

BREED BOX

Length	15 cm (6 in)
Incubation period	13 days
Fledging period	27 days
Clutch size	4–6 eggs

AUSTRALIAN GRASSFINCHES

This group of finches includes highly coloured birds such as the Gouldian and parrot finches. A number of species are commonly bred, and they are easy birds to look after, although foster parents may be needed to hatch and rear the chicks. Cage-breeding is practised with Australian grassfinches, which has helped to establish colour varieties: pairings can be controlled to maximize the chance of young of a specific colour.

PARROTFINCHES

The most widely bred species is the blue-faced parrotfinch (*Erythrura trichroa*) from New Guinea. The blue on the sides of the head is less evident in hens.

A commercial foreign finch seed mix, augmented with greenstuff, egg food and

◆ BELOW
This is a true pair of blue-faced parrotfinches, but separating the sexes by sight is very difficult. Young birds moult into adult plumage at about five months old, showing little sign of blue feathering on their heads up to this point.

BREED BOX

Length	13 cm (5 in)
Incubation period	14 days
Fledging period	23 days
Clutch size	4–5 eggs

small livefoods, is recommended once the chicks have hatched. Soaked seed, especially millet sprays, is valuable at this time as well. Pairs can be nervous and are most likely to nest in a planted flight, where they may rear two rounds of chicks in rapid succession.

GOULDIAN FINCHES

Australia is home to a group of finches that rivals the parrotfinches in colour. The Gouldian finch (*Chloebia gouldiae*) is unusual in that it occurs in three head colours in the wild – red, black and yellow (in reality, more of an orange tone). Hens are paler than cock birds, which develop a reddish tip to the bill as they come into breeding condition. Such is the interest in Gouldian finches that a number of distinctive colour varieties have been created. These can affect the head coloration or the plumage on the breast or the body, and sometimes the entire body. Among the most popular variants are the white-breasted and lilac-breasted forms, along with the blue-backed, although many breeders still regard the natural colours as the most attractive.

In spite of having been bred for many generations, these beautiful finches need to be kept warm, and they must be overwintered in heated accommodation in temperate areas.

Pairs are usually put in cages to breed. Some breeders keep Bengalese as well as Gouldian finches, in case foster parents are needed. Gouldian finches are susceptible to air-sac mites, minute parasites that live in the airways, and these interfere with their breathing, causing wheezing and loss of condition. It is possible to treat cases of air-sac mite with ivermectin, but it is also necessary to break the cycle of transmission. Adult birds pass the mites to their chicks when they feed them; by fostering the eggs before they hatch, there will be no risk of the young Gouldians

♦ ABOVE
The Gouldian finch is often called Lady Gould's finch in North America. It was named by the Victorian explorer John Gould after his wife Elizabeth because of its stunning beauty. This is the black-headed form.

♦ LEFT
The orange- or yellow-headed Gouldian finch is the rarest variety in the wild. It is the dilute form of the red-headed.

being infected, provided that they are subsequently kept away from any older birds that could be carrying the parasites.

Gouldian chicks are very drab compared with adult birds. They acquire their adult plumage from the age of about six weeks onwards, and

BREED BOX

Length	13 cm (5 in)
Incubation period	14 days
Fledging period	21 days
Clutch size	4–5 eggs

this can be a difficult time for them. It is important not to wean the chicks too early, as this may increase the risk of them suffering from the condition often described as "going light", that is, weight loss across the breastbone. It may be caused by the birds not eating enough to maintain their body weight, or it could be the result of an infection. If you have the misfortune to start losing Gouldian chicks, it is important to have the birds autopsied so that the underlying cause can be identified and the remaining chicks can be treated.

♦ RIGHT
When male Gouldian finches, such as the red-headed one seen here, come into breeding condition, cock birds develop a cherry-red tip to their bills. The variety is genetically recessive to the black-headed form.

STAR FINCHES

Another Australian grassfinch well represented in bird-keeping circles is the star finch (*Neochmia ruficauda*), which is found on the eastern side of the continent. The white markings extending from the head, down the chest and on to the flanks are thought to resemble a star, hence its name. It is sometimes called the red-tailed grassfinch – red coloration is clearly visible on the rump and tail. Red plumage is also present on the head, merging with the bright red colour of the bill.

The hen's head colour is paler than the cock bird's, but this is not an entirely reliable guide because young birds of both sexes are similarly coloured. Pairs may nest in a breeding cage equipped with a nest box or in aviary surroundings, where they prefer to construct their own nest. Expect two or even three rounds of up to four chicks each to be reared in succession.

BREED BOX

Length	10 cm (4 in)
Incubation period	13 days
Fledging period	21 days
Clutch size	4–6 eggs

♦ BELOW
In this pair of star finches, the subdued colour of the hen contrasts with the more brightly coloured cock. These grassfinches will usually rear their young on soft food, so there is no need to provide small invertebrates for them.

MASKED GRASSFINCHES

✦ LEFT
Visual sexing is
virtually impossible
for masked
grassfinches. These
birds prefer a well-
planted aviary that
provides them with
seclusion if danger
threatens.

The masked grassfinch (*Poephila personata*) originates from northern and eastern parts of Australia. The mask is a distinctive shade of black, with the wings and underparts being predominantly brown. White and black areas of plumage are present on the rear of the body. The cock's song is the best way of distinguishing the sexes.

Feeding requirements are basically identical to those of other finches, but they do not necessarily need invertebrates to rear their chicks.

Masked grassfinches are lively and rather nervous by nature; breeding successes are more likely in flights than in cages. It is worthwhile keeping a few pairs of Bengalese so the grassfinches' eggs can be fostered if the nest is abandoned.

In common with other related Australian species, it is a good idea to provide them with a source of granulated charcoal. The finches use this as a deodorizer, scattering it in the bottom of the nest. No one knows why this strange behaviour has arisen – one theory is that it may deter flies from the nest site.

BREED BOX

Length	13 cm (5 in)
Incubation period	13 days
Fledging period	21 days
Clutch size	4–5 eggs

ZEBRA FINCHES

The most widely kept of the Australian finches is the zebra finch (*P. guttata*), so-called because of the black and white stripes on the sides of the cock bird's body. The hen is duller by comparison, although some have white feathering. The sexes can also be distinguished by the bill – the cock bird's is a brighter red.

The first dark-eyed white mutation appeared in 1921. It can be separated from the chestnut-flanked white (often referred to as the "cfw") because cocks of this latter colour retain the characteristic markings on the sides of their bodies.

Pied zebra finches, i.e. ones that show both white and coloured areas in their

BREED BOX

Length	10 cm (4 in)
Incubation period	12 days
Fledging period	20 days
Clutch size	4–6 eggs

✦ ABOVE
The zebra-like markings of the cock zebra finch can be clearly seen in this individual. Hens are significantly duller in their overall colour.

plumage, are bred in a variety of colours – the pied mutation has been combined with other mutations such as the fawn, where the body colour is brownish rather than grey. In terms of solid colours, cream and silver forms have occurred, while more localized changes in coloration over recent years have led to the creation of varieties such as the orange-breasted and the black-breasted.

Mutations have not been confined to changes in colour. A crested form of the zebra finch can be linked with any colour. The crest forms a circular area of feathering in

the centre of the head. Rarer than this is the yellow-beaked variety, with the legs and feet also being paler in colour.

Zebra finches are easy birds to maintain. Their basic diet is mixed millets and canary seed, augmented with greenstuff and soft food. A vitamin and mineral supplement, sprinkled over the moist greenstuff, helps to compensate for the dietary deficiency in seed. Zebra finches live well in groups, and with other finches of similar size; they can also be housed with small doves and cockatiels. They are relatively hardy but they do need protection from the elements, so encourage them to roost in the aviary shelter, particularly when the weather is bad.

◆ ABOVE
The markings of the cock bird can be clearly seen in this exhibition pair of chestnut-flanked white zebra finches.

◆ ABOVE
In the fawn mutation of the zebra finch, it is easy to distinguish the sexes. The grey plumage has been replaced by a warmer shade of brown.

Pairs of Zebra finches will usually settle well in the home, although their constant cheeping can be a drawback. Outdoors, the cheeping is not loud enough to upset neighbours.

Pairs breed well in either aviary or cage surroundings, using a nest box or nesting basket. Once the pair have started to lay, do not provide further nesting material; they may start to build over their eggs. Chicks should start to hatch after approximately 12 days, and fledge when they are about three weeks old. Adult birds may lay two or even three clutches in rapid succession; remove nesting facilities at this stage to prevent them from becoming overtaxed.

The young mature from about three months onwards, but it is not a good idea to allow them to breed until they are at least six months of age and fully mature.

◆ LEFT AND RIGHT
Note the black area of plumage in the cock bird of this pair of black-breasted zebra finches.

WEAVERS AND WHYDAHS

Weavers will often develop amazingly colourful plumage at the onset of the breeding season. Cock whydah birds can be recognized by their magnificent tail plumes, and are known as widow birds because black predominates in their plumage at this time of the year. Whydahs and weavers are frequently polygamous, their plumage serving to attract harems of hens. Cock weaver birds construct the most ornate nests in aviary surroundings, just as they do in the wild, when provided with suitable materials such as dried grass and thin twigs. Whydahs often do not bother to build a nest; the hens seek out particular waxbills' nests and lay their eggs there, taking no part in the rearing of their offspring.

◆ OPPOSITE
The male red bishop undergoes a striking transformation in appearance at the start of the breeding season. For the remainder of the year, his plumage is drab.

◆ ABOVE LEFT
The village weaver is an active, robust bird that is easy to keep and quite hardy, once acclimatized. Cock birds weave ornate nests to attract potential mates.

WEAVERS

The weaver group is so-called because of the way the cock birds construct their ornate nests, weaving them from strands of grass and other foliage materials. Nests are often suspended from bushes, or even from the aviary mesh itself. Weavers make fascinating aviary occupants, although they are not suitable companions for smaller birds, such as waxbills. For successful breeding, house the cocks in the company of several hens rather than in pairs.

RED BISHOPS

The red bishop (*Euplectes orix*) is one of the most spectacular members of the weaver group. Cock birds develop a magnificent ruff of brilliant orange plumage around the neck when they come into breeding condition, and this is offset against the black feathering elsewhere on the body. The mantle over the back is of a browner

◆ LEFT
The cock bird of this pa[ir]
of orange weavers is in
his breeding plumage.
Colour feeding at the
time of the moult can
help to maintain the
intensity of the orange
feathering, although thi[s]
is not always necessary.

BREED BOX

Length	15 cm (6 in)
Incubation period	14 days
Fledging period	15 days
Clutch size	2–7 eggs

shade, with orange around the vent. Hens, in comparison, are basically brown in colour, with some darker streaking, especially on the underparts. There are a number of different forms of the red bishop species, which ranges widely across much of northern Africa, to the south of the Sahara.

A planted aviary is recommended for breeding, and will provide the cock with plenty of opportunity to weave its nests. It is important to keep two or three hens with each cock – a single hen is likely to be persecuted by her would-be suitor, and this will make successful breeding unlikely.

VILLAGE WEAVERS

The village weaver (*Ploceus cucullatus*) has very similar requirements to the red bishop. Cocks develop rich yellowish underparts offset against a blackish head when in breeding condition. When out of colour, they resemble hens, but with more black streaking on their bodies. It is advisable to keep cock birds apart because they may fight, especially during the breeding period. Hens lay clutches of up to four eggs, which should hatch after a fortnight. The young leave the nest at two weeks old.

BREED BOX

Length	17.5 cm (7 in)
Incubation period	14 days
Fledging period	15 days
Clutch size	2–4 eggs

◆ LEFT
The male village weaver's strong,
conical bill helps these birds to build
their nests effectively, acting rather
like a sewing needle. The bill can also
be used to devastating effect to bully
smaller companions.

RED-BILLED WEAVERS

In spite of being one of the commonest birds in the world, successful breedings of the

BREED BOX

Length	13 cm (5 in)
Incubation period	14 days
Fledging period	18 days
Clutch size	2–4 eggs

red-billed weaver (*Quelea quelea*) in aviary surroundings are unusual. The red-billed weaver needs to be housed in large flocks to stimulate breeding activity, with strong bonds forming between individual pairs in the group.

♦ LEFT
The attractive colour of the male weaver's breeding plumage is clearly shown here in contrast with the hen. The male bird's feet, too, are more brightly coloured.

When not in breeding condition, the colour of the hen's bill is yellowish rather than red. The cock bird's bill is always red, and his body colouring, from the plumage to the feet, will differentiate him from the hen.

WHYDAHS

The breeding requirements of these birds are specialized, but otherwise they are easy to keep. Cock birds are often advertised with the letters "IFC" after the name, indicating that they are in full colour at this time.

♦ FAR RIGHT
The amazing appearance of the male Fischer's whydah, with its elongated tail plumes, has led to these birds sometimes being known as straw-tailed whydahs.

FISCHER'S WHYDAHS

Fischer's whydah (*Vidua fischeri*), from East Africa, is a typical example of this group. The tail feathers of the cock bird grow to a length of 20 cm (8 in), which is approximately double that of its body. Hen birds usually lay their eggs in the nests of the purple grenadier waxbill (*Uraeginthus ianthinogaster*), a relative of the cordon bleu, or the red-eared waxbill. Some of these birds must therefore be housed with Fischer's whydahs in a large aviary if breeding is to be successful.

BREED BOX

Length	10 cm (4 in)
Incubation period	12 days
Fledging period	21 days
Clutch size	3 eggs

SENEGAL COMBASSOUS

The Senegal combassou or village indigo bird (*V. chalybeata*) uses the nests of the Senegal firefinch for its eggs, but if a cock is housed with several hens in an aviary on their own, the hens may construct their own nests.

BREED BOX

Length	13 cm (5 in)
Incubation period	12 days
Fledging period	14 days
Clutch size	3 eggs

♦ LEFT AND ABOVE
A cock Senegal combassou moults into breeding plumage by shedding its lighter coloured feathers. The resulting dark blue colour is why these whydahs are also known as village indigo birds.

CANARIES AND RELATED FINCHES

Canaries are descended from finches that live on the Canary islands, off the west coast of Africa, and after over 500 years of selective breeding, cage and aviary varieties are far removed from their wild relatives. The characteristic that first attracted people to the canary was the singing ability of the cock birds. This is at its best in the springtime at the start of the breeding period, but the birds sing throughout the year, except during the moult, which occurs after the breeding season in late summer.

♦ OPPOSITE

A pair of green singing finches. These birds are less distinct in colour than their close relation, the canary, and, in spite of their name, they sing less well; they are less popular as pets as a result.

♦ ABOVE LEFT

The Fife fancy is one of the group of type canaries, bred primarily for its appearance rather than its singing prowess. They are available in a wide range of colours.

CANARIES

The canary's early development took place in the Harz Mountain area of Germany. The birds were valued for their song, and young cock birds were trained to mimic the sound of the mountain streams of the region. This tradition is still reflected in the show bird standard. The origins of other varieties, bred for looks and posture, can be traced back to Holland and Belgium. From there, they spread to different localities in Europe and the breeds evolved in isolation. This is reflected in the breed names, which echo the area where they were developed. For instance, an influx of Flemish refugees, fleeing religious persecution in Belgium, led to the development of the Norwich canary in the East Anglia region of England. These chunky birds are still seen in shows in that area.

It is fashion that dictates a breed's rise or fall in popularity. The Scotch fancy was common in Scotland in Victorian times but is now scarce. As a posture breed, the bird's shape had made it popular, but the form had to be adopted at shows, and the difficulty in training the birds became a factor in their decline when tastes moved on.

BREED BOX

Length	10.5–20 cm (4¹/₊–8 in)
Incubation period	14 days
Fledging period	14 days
Clutch size	4 eggs

✦ ABOVE
Wild canaries are far less colourful than their domesticated relatives. In fact, they are very rarely kept outside their native islands.

✦ LEFT
The green singing finch (*Serinus mozambicus*), a close relative of the canary, is found over a wide area of mainland Africa, and has an attractive song. It needs similar care in aviary surroundings. Hens can be identified by the black spots across the throat. They have been known to live for 20 years or more.

Among the most popular international breeds today are the Border fancy, which was developed in the Border district between England and Scotland, and its smaller compatriot, the Fife fancy, which was developed as a result of concerns that the Border was becoming too large.

Another newcomer with an established following is the Gloster, a breed created in the 1920s in the English county of Gloucestershire by crossing crested roller and Border fancy canaries. As the result of the lethal factor associated with crested mutations, crested birds are not paired together but with non-crested individuals. The crested form of the Gloster is called the corona, the non-crested form, the consort. These birds are bred in a wide range of colours, including green, blue (which is actually a greyish variant) and white, as well as variegated forms.

Many breeds have changed in appearance down the centuries. The Yorkshire fancy, which was developed in the coal mining communities of northern England, used to be popularly regarded as slim enough to slip through a wedding ring, and early illustrations from the 1850s portray these

◆ ABOVE
The stocky build of the Norwich is the reason these canaries are sometimes called the John Bull of the canary fancy, after the popular figure of English folklore. This particular canary is a buff-feathered hen.

◆ RIGHT
This example of a top Border fancy canary shows the relatively small, rounded head, as well as the rounded back and chest that are characteristic of the breed. The wing tips meet at the base of the back.

◆ LEFT
This curved posture is the typical stance of the Scotch fancy. The way the bird holds its head forward emphasizes the length of its neck. When being exhibited in a show cage, these canaries hop back and forth in a characteristic manner, keeping their wings closed. This movement is called "travelling".

◆ LEFT
This Fife fancy canary shows the typical yellow colour that is closely associated with these birds, although canaries are bred in a wide range of colours. The lack of any dark markings on its body means that it is described as a clear yellow.

◆ RIGHT
The crest of the Gloster corona should be even, and must not obscure the eyes. The neck should be relatively thick. This is a variegated bird, which has both dark and light areas in its plumage.

◆ BELOW
The Gloster consort matches the corona in all respects, apart from its lack of a crest. This particular individual is described as three parts dark because of the extent of the variegation in its plumage.

canaries as being very thin but tall. Today, although the Yorkshire has retained its stature, sometimes being dubbed the "guardsman of the fancy", it has become a heavier breed.

The oldest and undoubtedly the most unusual breed of canary is the lizard. Its origins have been lost, but the earliest published account of canary variants, published in the early 1700s, lists birds with very similar markings. It got its name from the rows of markings running down the sides of its body, which approximate to the scales of a reptile. Lizards may have a clear area of plumage on the head, called a cap. If this is complete, the bird is described as clear-capped, but if it is divided up with darker feathering, it is called broken-capped. Those lizards without caps are known as non-capped.

HYBRID CANARIES

There are those who believe that the lizard is not of pure canary descent, and suggest that it may have been hybridized with a native finch early in its development. They point to the fact that its markings are highly unusual, and cite the development of the red factor canary as evidence that such crosses can be made successfully. This radical change in the canary's colour came about in the 1920s, as a result of a breeding experiment with the aim of creating canaries with pure red feathering. It provided the stimulus for the development of what are often termed "coloured canaries".

The red coloration was introduced as the result of crossings between canaries and a related finch, the black-hooded red siskin (*Carduelis cucullata*), that inhabits the northern part of South America. The resulting hybrids proved fertile, and so it was possible to create a strain of such birds, but they still retain an orange shade to their plumage rather than being pure red, and the distinction between the two feather types that exist in all canaries is clearly evident. Generally, the buff form is described as frosted, compared with the non-frosted (yellow) variety. This is a reflection of the distribution of colour

◆ RIGHT

This beautiful clear yellow Yorkshire fancy canary shows the height of these birds. They must adopt an upright stance in the show cage with no tendency to slouch. Yorkshire canaries measure approximately 17 cm (6¹/₂ in) long.

◆ BELOW

This is a clear-capped lizard canary. These birds are described as having a silver feather type, corresponding to buff in most other breeds. The yellow-feathered counterpart in the lizard is known as the gold.

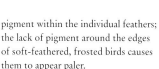

FEATHER LUMPS

The characteristic known as feather lumps has become a problem for the Gloster as well as for the Norwich canary. Feather lumps are caused by the repeated pairings of buff-feathered birds – a process called double buffing – in order to increase their overall size. The practice can result in the plumage becoming so soft that feathers cannot emerge properly from their shafts. The feathers will actually grow back under the bird's skin, causing painful and unsightly swellings that do eventually drop off, although recurrences over successive moults are common. The long-term solution to prevent feather lumps is to incorporate birds of yellow, rather than buff, feather type into the breeding programme.

Norwich canaries with lumps can be used to produce mules. The risk of feather lumps makes the Norwich birds unsuitable for breeding with each other, but using them in this way means the characteristic will not be passed on.

◆ BELOW

Black-hooded red siskins were used in the development of the red factor canary. They are kept in their own right and require similar care to canaries, but they are scarce in aviculture and strictly protected in the wild. The hen is far less colourful than the cock, but this characteristic is not seen in their canary descendants, for which sexing depends on the cock's song.

pigment within the individual feathers; the lack of pigment around the edges of soft-feathered, frosted birds causes them to appear paler.

Domestic canaries have been crossed with any number of other finches to produce hybrids. When a canary is bred with a European finch, such as a goldfinch, the resulting offspring are described as mules. Mules are valued for their appearance or song, but development of a strain is impossible because they are normally infertile. It is usual practice to pair a hen canary with a cock finch because the canary will prove to be a steadier parent.

◆ ABOVE
The hens originally bred from pairings between canaries and black-hooded red siskins were infertile until the third generation. Today, the fertility of red canaries such as this intensive clear red is normal.

FEEDING

Canaries are straightforward to look after, with few special requirements, although they can be very wasteful in their feeding habits. The main ingredients in their seed mix are red rape and plain canary seed, augmented with other items such as niger, gold of pleasure, hemp and linseed. Greenstuff such as chickweed should be offered regularly, along with egg food, particularly when the birds are breeding. Provide greenstuff regularly in small amounts, rather than only occasionally in large amounts, to avoid any risk of causing diarrhoea.

During the moulting period, a slightly different diet is required, because this is when new feathers will take up colour pigments. Red factor canaries should be offered a diet based mainly on groats and niger, rather than a regular canary seed mix, to reduce the uptake of yellow pigment into their plumage, which will turn it a shade of orange. Egg food should be withheld and a colouring agent administered via the drinking water at this time.

Colour feeding will improve the intensity of the bird's coloration, but it is not permitted for all breeds. Liquid colour agents and soft foods produced for this purpose are available from birdseed suppliers and pet stores. Be sure to follow the manufacturer's instructions exactly – overdosing on liquid colour will spoil the appearance of the bird's plumage until the next moult. This will mean a disastrous showing season, and you may unwittingly put the bird's health at risk.

BREEDING

Pair up canaries in the spring, and provide each pair with a nesting pan lined with felt stitched in at the bottom. Make sure nesting material is available. Move the cock bird to another location after a fortnight; he plays no further part in the breeding process. It is standard practice to remove the eggs as they are laid,

◆ ABOVE
The new colour canary group consists of many different varieties. Colour is the paramount feature. This particular individual is an intensive rose bronze, with the bronze input darkening the bird's plumage.

◆ LEFT
Mules are popular exhibition subjects. This particular lightly marked goldfinch mule won the overall supreme award out of nearly 10,000 birds of all varieties entered at the British National Exhibition of Cage & Aviary Birds. More mules have presently achieved this honour than either canaries or budgerigars, in spite of their relative scarcity.

◆ LEFT
Aviary-bred goldfinches are very
popular for breeding mules because
of their colourful appearance. They
will usually mate readily with hen
canaries if they are paired together
on their own.

replacing them with dummy eggs. On
the fourth morning, put back the three
eggs laid previously and remove the
substitutes. This ensures that the
chicks hatch together, approximately
13 days later, increasing their chances
of survival. If the chicks are to be
close-rung, this should take place
at six days old: the circular band can
be slid up their legs over the toes.

During the breeding period, even
before the chicks have hatched, a
regular supply of egg food should be

◆ BELOW
The Parisian frill is one of the
largest of all canaries, measuring
approximately 20 cm (8 in) in
length. The distinctive pattern of
the feathering is set down in the
show standard for the breed.

offered to the hen. Pre-mixed egg
foods are a better option than those
which need to be mixed with water,
because they are of a standard
consistency. Provide a fresh supply
once or twice daily, in a clean
container. Most hens produce two
rounds of chicks in succession.
Reintroduce the cock bird when
the young are roughly 18 days old,
and provide a second nesting pan.

Once the chicks start to feed on
their own, sprinkle tiny blue maw seed
on top of the egg food to help wean
them on to seed. Soaked seed is
valuable at this stage, being softer than
seed straight from a packet, although
any prepared in this way must be
discarded at the end of the day,
particularly in hot weather, before it
turns mouldy. Young canaries can
usually be removed from the breeding
cage when they are three weeks old.
They often live for nine years or more,
and sometimes for over 15 years. The
young birds should be transferred to
an indoor flight at first, before being
released into an outdoor aviary when
the weather is good.

◆ ABOVE
Canaries with frilled plumage are popular in
mainland Europe, where there are a number of
distinctive varieties. The North Dutch frill is
considered to be the ancestor of all today's
frilled breeds. Red coloration has been
introduced to this breed, creating canaries with
a very distinctive appearance. They need to be
colour-fed.

QUAILS AND PHEASANTS

This group of birds is quite nervous by nature, and so will benefit from being kept in a planted aviary environment. They can also be highly aggressive, with the colourful plumage of cock birds actually serving as a threat to other males of their own kind, which is why they must be kept strictly apart from each other. Screening between adjacent aviaries at eye-level is particularly vital, to prevent the birds from attempting to fight through the double layer of mesh separating them. They are often housed in trios comprising a cock and two hens, rather than in pairs. A single hen may end up being persecuted by her mate, to the extent that the pair have to be separated to safeguard her health.

♦ OPPOSITE
The magnificent display of the cock Indian
peafowl is one of the most amazing sights
in the natural world. These birds need
plenty of space and are surprisingly noisy.

♦ ABOVE
Pheasants will spend much of their time
on the ground and need to be housed in
planted aviaries, which offer them a good
amount of seclusion.

QUAILS

The quail group of birds will live happily on the floor of the aviary. An opening cut at low level, allowing the birds to move easily from the shelter into the flight and back, ensures the quails can seek protection from the elements when necessary, and is therefore very important. Such an opening can be easily fitted in the main door. Quails should be given their food inside the shelter for the extra protection offered; special quail feeders prevent the birds from scattering their food around on the floor. Small seeds, notably assorted millets, should form the basis of their diet, augmented with livefood such as small mealworms and soft food.

Quails are relatively hardy birds but they dislike damp conditions, and it is important that their quarters are well-drained to avoid risk of flooding. A concrete base is not entirely suitable because the birds are likely to suffer calluses on their feet from walking constantly over a hard and potentially abrasive surface. Coarse gravel is a more suitable option; it helps to have an area of grass in the flight as well, where the birds can scratch around, and to incorporate plants for cover. These conditions encourage successful breeding, although it is often the case that quails ignore their eggs, which must then be transferred to an incubator for hatching.

CHINESE PAINTED QUAILS

The Chinese painted quail (*Coturnix chinensis*), often referred to as CPQ, is the most widely kept species of quail. These birds measure just 13 cm (5 in) in length and will not disturb other birds, even small finches, when sharing their quarters. They show far less tendency to fly than others of the species, and do not seek to perch off the ground. In spite of their small size, male Chinese painted quails can be very aggressive. It is advisable to keep them in small groups rather than in pairs, running a cock with at least two and up to four hens. A single hen will be persecuted by her intended mate,

BREED BOX	
Length	13 cm (5 in)
Incubation period	18 days
Fledging period	not applicable
Clutch size	7–10 eggs

particularly at the onset of the breeding season, and will probably be severely feather-plucked.

The chicks are tiny, not much bigger than bumble bees, and are able to run around almost immediately after hatching. Egg food and blue maw seed is the rearing food, along with soaked millet sprays.

Several colour forms of the Chinese painted quail have been established; the most commonly kept is the silver variant – birds of both sexes have a distinctly silvery tone to their plumage but they can still be sexed easily.

◆ LEFT
In this pair of Chinese painted quails, the cock can be distinguished by its blue and reddish-chestnut coloration, while the hen is brownish.

JAPANESE QUAILS

The Japanese quail (*Coturnix coturnix*) is slightly larger in size than the Chinese painted, but similar in its requirements. These quails have been bred in a range of different strains as domestication has occurred.

BREED BOX

Length	17.5 cm (7 in)
Incubation period	18 days
Fledging period	not applicable
Clutch size	12 eggs

◆ ABOVE

Like other quails, hatching eggs in incubators over many generations has adversely affected the parenting instincts of Japanese quail, to the extent that they may be reluctant to incubate their own eggs.

BOBWHITE QUAILS

The bobwhite quail (*Colinus virginanus*) from North America is an attractive species, measuring about 23 cm (9 in) in length. It is important to remember that these quails are rather nervous birds and their aviary must be designed accordingly to ensure their safety. If alarmed, they will fly up almost vertically, which means that not only may they badly injure their heads on the roof of their quarters, but they can also cause other aviary birds above them to panic, with potentially fatal consequences.

BREED BOX

Length	23 cm (9 in)
Incubation period	21 days
Fledging period	not applicable
Clutch size	12–20 eggs

◆ ABOVE

The male bobwhite quail shown here has brighter markings than the hen, with more whitish areas on the head.

ORNAMENTAL PHEASANTS

These magnificent birds look truly spectacular when housed in spacious aviary surroundings, but bear in mind that cocks are particularly aggressive and should not be housed together. In fact, it is not a good idea to keep pheasants of the same species in adjacent flights because the cock birds will try to reach each other through the mesh. Double-wiring on both sides of the aviary framework will help to prevent direct physical contact. It would also be worthwhile to build up the base of the aviary, so that there is a solid barrier extending up the sides. This will discourage aggression by ensuring that the birds cannot see their neighbours.

LADY AMHERST'S PHEASANTS

Among the most widely kept species of pheasant is Lady Amherst's (*Chrysolophus amherstiae*), which is known to originate from China, Tibet and Myanmar (formerly Burma). The cock bird is particularly striking in appearance, thanks to its red, metallic green, blue, white and barred feathering; the hen is duller in coloration. Like most other pheasant species, these birds are polygamous so, when breeding, a cock bird should be kept in the company of two or three hens in a well-planted flight which allows the females sufficient shelter and space to incubate their eggs. Each clutch comprises 10 or more eggs. Should a hen refuse to sit, the eggs can be transferred under a broody bantam, which will usually hatch the eggs satisfactorily without any problems.

BREED BOX

Length	173 cm (68 in)
Incubation period	23 days
Fledging period	not applicable
Clutch size	10–12 eggs

◆ BELOW
The beautiful Lady Amherst's pheasant is named after the wife of a British ambassador. When displaying, the cock bird spreads his collar to emphasize the colour of his mantle.

GOLDEN PHEASANTS

The golden pheasant (*Chrysolophus pictus*) is perhaps even more spectacular in appearance than Lady Amherst's. Shades of gold, orange and chestnut-red, along with browns and metallic green areas, dominate in the case of mature cock birds of this species. They are smaller than Lady Amherst's, with cock birds averaging up to about 112 cm (44 in) in length. Hens are mainly brown in colour. Young male golden pheasants resemble hens, and it is likely to take two years for cock birds to develop their breeding finery.

The incubation period lasts for about 23 days, with hens laying in a scrape on the ground. Once the chicks have hatched, smaller seeds such as

♦ RIGHT
The golden pheasant is one of the most widely kept of all pheasants. Breeding may be best accomplished by introducing the cock to the quarters of the hens and removing him once egg-laying begins, to minimize the risk of aggression.

millets should be provided, along with starter crumbs and some livefood. Feeding the adult birds is completely straightforward; a pheasant seed mix is ideal and they will also eat greenstuff and invertebrates.

A variety of colour mutations includes Gighi's yellow golden pheasant, named in part after the Italian professor who helped to establish it. It is, in effect, a dilute mutation with the overall intensity of the colour being reduced.

Dark-throated and salmon varieties have also been developed but are not very widely kept.

BREED BOX

Length	112 cm (44 in)
Incubation period	23 days
Fledging period	not applicable
Clutch size	10–12 eggs

HIMALAYAN MONALS

In terms of iridescence, few birds have more striking plumage than the cock Himalayan monal (*Lophophorus impleyanus*). Bronze, blue, green and gold are just some of the colours that are apparent. Hens are very easy to identify by their streaked brownish coloration, with a white area of feathering under the throat. Originating from reasonably high altitudes, Himalayan monals are used

♦ RIGHT
This pair of Himalayan monals demonstrates that, as with most pheasants, these birds can be sexed easily, although it is often possible to confuse young birds of both sexes with the adult hens.

BREED BOX

Length	71 cm (28 in)
Incubation period	27 days
Fledging period	not applicable
Clutch size	5–6 eggs

to cold weather but dislike prolonged damp, dank conditions. A large, densely planted enclosure reduces the risk of a serious attack on the hen by her intended mate, while also giving her greater security in which to raise her offspring.

The clutches are rarely of more than six eggs and, as a result, breeders often remove the first clutch soon after laying, with the aim of encouraging the hen to lay again soon afterwards. Incubation takes around 27 days and the young are able to walk almost immediately after hatching. In the case of birds in immature plumage, look for traces of black feathering on the throat; this indicates a young cock. It takes two years for these birds to acquire full adult plumage.

SOFTBILLS

The name of this large and diverse group of birds derives not from the texture of their bills – which are not soft and may inflict a painful bite if the bird manages to grab hold of a finger – but from their nutritional needs, in that hard seed does not feature in their diet. Softbills are fed on softbill mix, as well as on fruit, invertebrates and, in some cases, nectar. The housing needs of softbills can vary widely, but the size of the birds gives a valuable insight into their relative hardiness. Smaller individuals, such as sugarbirds, are not sufficiently hardy to live outdoors throughout the year in temperate areas, and will require additional heating and lighting through the winter period. Softbills can be kept as part of a mixed collection, but they may not always agree amongst themselves; much will depend on the species concerned.

◆ OPPOSITE
Levaillant's barbet is an attractive African bird easily maintained on a diet of fruit, insects and softbill food. Like most softbills, these are aviary rather than pet birds.

◆ ABOVE LEFT
Touracos are unusual softbills in that they feed to a large extent on plant matter. Caring for softbills takes more time than finches because of their dietary needs.

SMALL SOFTBILLS

Softbills are a very diverse group of birds. They are distinguished in terms of their dietary needs rather than their zoology – their bills are not actually soft – and there are three recognized sub-divisions, based on the dietary requirements of the different species. There are the nectivores, which rely mainly on nectar to meet their nutritional needs; the frugivores, feeding largely on fruit; and the insectivores, which eat mainly invertebrates. These categories serve only as a general indication of feeding requirements; all softbills require a wide variety of foodstuffs in order to remain in good health and to breed successfully.

The size of these birds is significant in terms of their care. The smaller softbills are less hardy than larger members of this group and will always require heated winter accommodation in temperate areas. Additional lighting, to extend the feeding period to twelve hours, will be important in latitudes where shortened daylight hours occur throughout the winter.

A planted aviary is recommended, and they must have a water container or small pool for bathing purposes, as well as separate water for drinking. Good hygiene is vital for nectivores in particular; sour nectar can rapidly cause serious intestinal upsets. Dirty drinkers are likely to give rise to the fungal infection known as candidiasis. An affected individual will often hold its bill ajar, and a cheesy growth within, a characteristic of the infection, is evident on closer inspection. Treatments include using a specific anti-fungal preparation, but beware because an outbreak can spread rapidly from drinkers.

SUNBIRDS

The requirements of hummingbirds may be too specialized for most bird-keepers, although some dedicated fanciers do keep and breed them successfully, but there are a number of other attractive nectivores that are more straightforward to care for. The sunbirds, for example, are often considered to be the Old World hummingbirds' equivalents. They share a number of characteristics, including iridescence on their plumage in many cases, and long, narrow, pointed bills to probe into flowers for nectar. However, sunbirds cannot feed in flight while hovering, but must perch for this purpose. Sunbirds found in Asia have a reputation for being difficult to keep because they are more insectivorous in their feeding habits than some of their African relatives.

In most cases, sexing is relatively straightforward because cocks are usually more brightly coloured than hens. The difficulty stems from identifying the species or age of hens

♦ RIGHT
In breeding plumage, the cock malachite sunbird is a magnificent dark green, whereas the hen is olive-brown above with yellowish grey underparts. Out of colour, the cock can still be recognized by his two elongated central tail feathers.

correctly; in most cases they are all very similar. It helps to refer to a specialist field guide with coloured photographs showing the prime distinguishing features of species.

BREED BOX

Length	15 cm (6 in)
Incubation period	14 days
Fledging period	14 days
Clutch size	1 egg

MALACHITE SUNBIRDS

The malachite sunbird (*Nectarinia famosa*) is one of the most distinctive African species, with the long tail feathers of the cock bird accounting for about half its total length of 15 cm (6 in). Like others of their type, these sunbirds feed on a diet of nectar, and small insects such as young crickets; sometimes the birds will take a fine-grade insectivorous food and sponge cake soaked in nectar.

In aviary surroundings, the hen will build a large, suspended nest, often in a clump of bamboo, using a range of materials, including spiders' webs and moss. A single egg will be laid inside the nest. Young fledgling sunbirds are similar in size to their parents but they do have noticeably shorter bills.

◆ BELOW
Purple sugarbirds are relatively straightforward
to look after and, compared with sunbirds, are
easy to breed as well. They are keen bathers, like
most small nectivores.

PURPLE SUGARBIRDS

The purple sugarbird (*Cyanerpes caeruleus*) originates from northern parts of South America. It feeds mainly on nectar, although diced fruit and a fine-grade softbill food should also be provided daily, along with livefood such as crickets. Sexing is very easy – males are purple in colour whereas hens are mainly green. Young birds resemble hens, but odd purple

BREED BOX

Length	10 cm (4 in)
Incubation period	12 days
Fledging period	14 days
Clutch size	2 eggs

feathers on the head enable young cocks to be identified before they have fully moulted. Pairs may build a nest within a nesting basket or small nest box. There is a similar species

called the red-legged sugarbird (*Cyanerpes cyaneus*), the cocks of which only gain their purplish plumage for the duration of the breeding season.

BLUE DACNIS

The blue dacnis (*Dacnis cayana*) is found over a wide area of Central and South America. It has similar habits to the purple sugarbird, although its bill is shorter. Cocks are an attractive combination of blue and black, while hens are green. As in the case of other small softbills, these birds are not hardy and they will require protection from the elements.

◆ BELOW
In this pair of blue dacnis, the cock bird is on the right. Pairs
can be housed with other non-aggressive birds of similar size.
However, in a relatively small enclosure, they should be kept
apart from others of their kind because cocks may fight viciously.

BREED BOX

Length	13 cm (5 in)
Incubation period	12 days
Fledging period	14 days
Clutch size	2 eggs

TANAGERS

Tanagers are widely distributed in the Americas and are closely allied to the honeycreepers, although fruit rather than nectar is the mainstay of their diet. They are relatively easy to keep, eating a wide range of fruit and berries, and are quite able to use their stout bills to nibble chunks out of an apple rather than requiring it to be cut up into tiny pieces for them. Sprinkle a low-iron soft food over their fruit, which should be provided fresh each day along with a few invertebrates such as waxworms or mealworms.

Breeding is possible, particularly in a densely planted flight, but unfortunately, it is very difficult to sex tanagers visually. Cocks often have bolder heads than hens, but minor variations in appearance between individuals are likely to be due to them originating from different parts of their range.

Euphonias, such as the orange-crowned euphonia (*E. saturata*), are an offshoot of the main tanager group

+ RIGHT
Euphonias are small, stocky birds about 10 cm (4 in) long, and they have a pleasant song. This is a cock orange-crowned euphonia, from north-western South America.

BREED BOX

Length	10–20 cm (4–8 in)
Incubation period	15 days
Fledging period	19 days
Clutch size	2–5 eggs

and they can usually be sexed more easily. The cock is an attractive shade of violet, offset against rich yellow on the crown and underparts. Hens in comparison are predominantly greenish; an olive shade above and yellower on the underparts. They typically lay clutches of up to five eggs, and these should hatch after an incubation period of about 15 days. Livefood is important for rearing purposes, with the young fledgling feeding on its own at three weeks old.

+ ABOVE
Tanagers from high altitudes, such as the mountain species, are relatively hardy, but the smaller *Tangara* species such as the emerald spotted (*T. guttata*) require heat during the winter months.

✦ BELOW
Zosterops are lively, social birds that can be kept
in small groups or in the company of birds of
similar size. The chestnut-flanked variety
(*Z. erythropleura*) is often available.

ZOSTEROPS

The zosterops or white-eye (*Zosterops palpebrosa*) is one of a number of small softbills of Asiatic origin popular among bird-keepers. These birds need a constant supply of nectar as well as diced fruit, softbill food and small invertebrates. Like most nectivores, white-eyes are keen bathers and it is important that their liquid food is provided in a sealed container rather than an open pot; otherwise, the birds are likely to attempt to bathe in it and their plumage will inevitably become sticky as a result.

As the time for breeding approaches, cock birds start to sing and hens search for spiders' webs and other materials with which to construct their nests. The incubation and rearing periods last for about 12 days each and pairs may rear two clutches of chicks in rapid succession. Small livefoods such as crickets are necessary for the growth of the chicks. Zosterops must have snug winter-time accommodation, indoors out of the cold.

BREED BOX

Length	10 cm (4 in)
Incubation period	12 days
Fledging period	12 days
Clutch size	2–4 eggs

RED-HEADED TITS

Red-headed tits (*Aegithalos concinnus*) are another group of very active small softbills. They thrive on a varied diet but are insectivorous, so small crickets and fine-grade softbill food should feature prominently in their diet. Their small size and natural curiosity mean that they must have a fine covering of mesh over their flight, with no gaps, to prevent the possibility of escape. A planted flight suits them well, but these tits are not hardy and should be housed in warm surroundings during the winter time.

For breeding purposes, provide a small nest box or covered basket along with nesting material, sited in a well-planted area of the aviary. Pairs can be quite prolific. Hens lay up to six eggs in a clutch and they should hatch after a period of 14 days. Small livefoods such as aphids are necessary when the young are being reared.

BREED BOX

Length	10 cm (4 in)
Incubation period	14 days
Fledging period	14 days
Clutch size	5–6 eggs

✦ RIGHT
Red-headed tits are best kept in a group, certainly at first, if breeding is the aim. As visual sexing is impossible, this gives the best chance of obtaining at least one true pair.

BLACK-CHINNED YUHINAS

The black-chinned yuhina (*Yuhina nigramenta*) may not be as colourful as some softbills, but its attractive crest and lively personality help to compensate for that. These birds measure about 10 cm (4 in) long. Nectar, fruit diced into small pieces and small livefoods such as micro-crickets form the basis of their diet.

Yuhinas build a cup-shaped nest, well-hidden in vegetation. When displaying, the male lowers his crest and dances with his wings outstretched in front of the hen. Pairs are best housed away from others of their own kind because they persistently squabble at this stage of the year. Three eggs form a typical clutch, and this is incubated mainly

◆ RIGHT
This is a pair of black-chinned yuhinas. Males can be recognized when in breeding condition not just by their larger crests, but also by their song, although this is not very loud.

BREED BOX

Length	10 cm (4 in)
Incubation period	13 days
Fledging period	15 days
Clutch size	3–4 eggs

by the hen for 13 days. The young fledge after a similar interval. Small livefoods that can be easily digested by the chicks are vital for rearing purposes. Egg food should also be provided. When they leave the nest, the young are paler in colour than the adult birds.

PEKIN ROBINS

The pekin robin (*Leiothrix lutea*) has a wide distribution across southern parts of Asia. There may be minor differences in plumage between individuals and, unfortunately, there is no clear-cut way of distinguishing the

sexes by sight. Once in breeding condition, however, cocks have a magnificent song.

Pekin robins make an ideal introduction to keeping softbills. They are very easy to care for, taking a varied diet that may even include some millet seed. They are also relatively hardy once acclimatized, but must still have good protection during bad weather. Some provision for heating in their quarters is advisable. The main drawback of keeping pekin

◆ LEFT
In spite of its similarity in shape, the pekin robin is not actually a robin; nor is it confined to China. As well as insects, these birds eat large quantities of egg food when rearing their chicks.

BREED BOX

Length	15 cm (6 in)
Incubation period	14 days
Fledging period	14 days
Clutch size	4 eggs

robins in a mixed collection is that they can be disruptive during the breeding season, stealing the eggs of other birds that are sharing their accommodation. They build cup-shaped nests. The incubation and fledging periods last for about 14 days each. A pair may have more than one round of chicks in the summer, when the cock's melodious song will be frequently heard.

MEDIUM-SIZED SOFTBILLS

Not all softbills are colourful, but their interesting habits and attractive song compensate for lack of vivid plumage. Most of the species included in this section are relatively hardy, once properly acclimatized, but this may take a couple of years and it is important to have contingency plans in the event of severe weather – a flight attached to a well-insulated and heated birdroom, for instance. The birds can be shut inside, if necessary, although they do not need to be confined in cages. Softbills in general are very lively birds, and they will need to be housed in spacious surroundings if their feather condition is not to deteriorate through inadequate flight exercise.

GREATER HILL MYNAHS

The greater hill mynah (*Gracula religiosa*) is widely kept as a pet. Although unrivalled for the clarity of their speech, these members of the starling clan are messy by nature, and so are usually accommo- dated in box-type cages. It is important to start out with a young mynah as a pet. These are often advertised as "gapers" because of their habit of begging for food. They can be easily recognized by the flat, bare, yellow patches of skin on the sides of the head which are known as wattles; and their plumage lacks the iridescence of adults.

There are various subspecies of different sizes. Pairs can only be recognized with certainty by being sexed. Breeding is not too difficult. Provide a large nest box lined with twigs. The hen lays two or three eggs which hatch after 15 days. At this stage, the adult birds become much more insectivorous than usual, with the chicks ultimately fledging at about a month old. It is not uncommon for two clutches to be reared in succession. Early chicks should be removed when they are independent.

BREED BOX

Length	30 cm (12 in)
Incubation period	15 days
Fledging period	28 days
Clutch size	2–3 eggs

◆ LEFT
The powers of mimicry of the greater hill mynah may exceed those of parrots in some respects. They are less reluctant to talk in front of strangers, and also mimic sounds such as a ringing telephone with greater clarity.

MAGPIE ROBINS

Magpie robins (*Copsychus saularis*), also known as dhyal thrushes, are found across southern Asia and the Philippines. There are differences in markings between the various forms but generally adult cocks are a combination of black and white in colour, while hens display less contrast in their plumage and are greyer overall.

BREED BOX

Length	20 cm (8 in)
Incubation period	13 days
Fledging period	17 days
Clutch size	5 eggs

The melodic calls of the cock birds are most likely to be heard in the early morning and late afternoon, especially during the breeding season. The hen builds a cup-shaped nest, either directly in the vegetation of the flight, often favouring stands of bamboo, or in an open-fronted nest box. Magpie robins will often become very tame in aviary surroundings, especially when nesting, and many will be persuaded to take livefood from the hand. The hen will lay five eggs in a clutch. Incubation lasts for around 13 days and the young chicks will start to fledge from between two and three weeks after hatching.

♦ ABOVE
The immaculate appearance of the magpie robin, coupled with its fine song, has helped to make this species popular with softbill enthusiasts.

BLACK BULBULS

The black bulbul (*Hypsipetes madagascariensis*) is a typical representative of another not-very-colourful group of birds which, in the case of the cock bird, has an attractive song. This is the way to distinguish between the sexes. As the name indicates, these bulbuls are greyish-black in colour. In south-eastern Asia, there is a form which has a white head.

Although recognizing a pair is difficult at the outset, breeding is quite likely to take place, particularly in a planted aviary. A nest of twigs is constructed in the branches of a bush or tree, and lined with softer material. The hen sits alone, with the chicks hatching about 12 days later. The young leave the nest after about two weeks. Bulbuls are easy to cater for, taking a more

BREED BOX

Length	25 cm (10 in)
Incubation period	13 days
Fledging period	13 days
Clutch size	3–5 eggs

omnivorous diet than the magpie robin, including more finely chopped fruit and berries. Small livefoods such as crickets should be supplied during the rearing period, when egg food will also be taken. Bulbuls are reasonably peaceful by nature and can often be kept satisfactorily as part of a mixed collection. They are relatively hardy once acclimatized.

♦ LEFT
The black bulbul is one of the Asiatic species best known in bird-keeping circles, and is more widely kept than its African relatives. Their care is straightforward.

GREY LAUGHING THRUSHES

The laughing thrushes are so-called because of their calls, with some species proving to be talented songsters. They are a robust group of Asiatic softbills, popular in bird-keeping circles because they are hardy and easy to look after. They usually have to be housed on their own because of their predatory nature – hence their alternative name of jay thrush. The grey laughing thrush (*Garrulax maesi*) is a typical member of the group, recognizable by its silvery-grey ear coverts. It originates from southern and central areas of China, where it inhabits mountain forests. Unfortunately, there is no reliable way of distinguishing pairs visually, but their care is straightforward; a mixed diet including plenty of livefood, such as mealworms, suits them very well.

Dense bamboo undergrowth encourages breeding, with the birds becoming shyer at first during this period. Four eggs, hatching after 13 days, form a typical clutch. Keep disturbances to a minimum or the adult birds may eat their chicks.

BREED BOX

Length	28 cm (11 in)
Incubation period	13 days
Fledging period	21 days
Clutch size	4 eggs

◆ ABOVE
Laughing thrushes are highly active birds, bold and brash by nature. They can strike up a strong bond with their keeper in aviary surroundings. If housed as a group, beware that the weakest individual is not bullied by its companions.

Making them hunt for livefood by scattering it on the floor of the aviary may provide a distraction in the case of a pair known to attack their chicks.

BLACK-HEADED SIBIAS

The black-headed sibia (*Heterophasia capistrata*) originates in the Himalayan area of Asia, which makes it relatively hardy once settled in its surroundings. These sibias will thrive in a planted aviary and can become quite tame, often to the point of feeding on mealworms from the hand. Visual sexing is not possible, and this can be a major handicap to breeding attempts.

Conifers are a good choice of plant for sibias. They may even use pine needles to form the outer structure of their nests, lining the interior with softer materials. It will take about two weeks for the eggs to hatch, with the chicks leaving the nest after a similar period. Pairs are best housed on their own for breeding purposes, and should not be mixed with smaller companions who may be bullied, particularly when nesting is imminent.

BREED BOX

Length	25 cm (10 in)
Incubation period	14 days
Fledging period	14 days
Clutch size	4 eggs

◆ BELOW
The black-headed sibia cannot be sexed by sight, but breeding has proved possible in aviary surroundings. A pair is most likely to breed if housed on their own once they show signs of nesting behaviour.

LEVAILLANT'S BARBETS

◆ LEFT
The markings of Levaillant's barbets are highly individual, enabling the members of a pair to be distinguished without difficulty, once their genders have been accurately ascertained. These birds prefer to nest in logs rather than nest boxes.

Bill shape can give an indication of potential aggression, although in the case of barbets, their stocky bills have another important function – tunnelling into rotten wood or excavating nesting chambers in the ground. Even so, it is advisable to keep these attractive birds on their own, and never with smaller companions. Some can prove to be aggressive in the company of their own species. Sexing is difficult, although hens may be less brightly coloured overall.

Barbets form a large group, with distribution in parts of Africa, Asia and South America. It is important to find out the range of a particular species because this has a definite bearing on its requirements. Those from tropical forest areas are generally much more frigivorous in their feeding habits than those from the scrubland of southern Africa, such as Levaillant's barbet (*Trachyphonus vaillanti*), which take a more insectivorous diet.

A deep nest box, preferably covered with bark around the entrance hole, is recommended. The hen may lay up to five eggs, which take two weeks to hatch. Fledging occurs about three weeks later. A greatly increased supply of livefood is essential for rearing purposes, in addition to the regular offerings of fruit, berries and a low-iron softbill food or soaked mynah pellets.

Barbets need adequate protection from the cold and damp during the winter, and it is advisable to house them in a birdroom where heating and lighting are available through this period. Their strong bills can, however, inflict serious damage on woodwork.

BREED BOX

Length	20 cm (8 in)
Incubation period	14 days
Fledging period	22 days
Clutch size	3–5 eggs

SPECTACLED MOUSEBIRDS

Mousebirds are a group of African softbills that are highly social by nature and thrive in a well-planted flight, although they may damage some of the vegetation. The spectacled mousebird (*Colius striatus*) measures about 30 cm (12 in) overall, with its long tail accounting for approximately three-quarters of its total length.

There are a number of different subspecies, and there is no means of distinguishing the sexes visually.

Pairs build large, bulky nests, often well-disguised in vegetation, made of dry grass and moss. Three eggs form the typical clutch. They hatch in two weeks and the incubation is shared by both adult birds. The chicks develop very quickly and often leave the nest at about 10 days old, before they can fly, clambering around using their feet and bills. Mousebirds are very easy to feed on a diet of fruit, softbill food and berries, along with livefood and greenstuff such as chickweed. They are not hardy and need to be housed in warm, dry surroundings during the winter.

BREED BOX

Length	30 cm (12 in)
Incubation period	14 days
Fledging period	10 days
Clutch size	3 eggs

◆ RIGHT
A spectacled mousebird shows its climbing abilities. The coloration of these birds and the way in which they clamber quietly around the branches is the reason for their unusual common name.

LARGE SOFTBILLS

Unlike the smaller softbills, members of this group, especially those which originate from the more temperate latitudes, are relatively hardy after they have been properly acclimatized in their surroundings. However, all species will still require a heated, well-lit shelter during the colder winter months. A number of species of large softbill may be at risk from frost-bite in some climates, if they are allowed to remain out in the flight. Most large softbills are aggressive by nature, and should be accommodated in individual pairs rather than in large, mixed groups. Do not attempt to keep large softbill species in the company of smaller companions.

RED-BILLED TOUCANS

The toucans represent one of the best-known and most spectacular groups of larger softbills. They originate from parts of Central and South America. Thanks to a much better understanding of their needs in recent years, breeding success in private collections has become more commonplace. First and foremost, it is vital to use only a low-iron softbill food, or preferably softbill pellets, to safeguard against the premature demise of the birds from iron-storage disease. This is a dietary-induced illness which is almost impossible to cure by the time the symptoms have become apparent. Diced fruit should also figure prominently in their diet, along with livefood such as large crickets or mealworms, and even pinkie, or dead day old mice. Under no circumstances should pairs of toucans be housed with smaller companions, as these are likely to be seized and eaten.

It is not uncommon for a male toucan to persecute the hen intently at the start of the breeding period if she is not immediately responsive. It may be advisable to remove the male to separate accommodation until the hen is showing obvious signs of nesting activity. The red-billed toucan (*Ramphastos tucanus*) hen lays two or three eggs, incubating them for about 20 days. The young leave the nest at around eight weeks of age. A varied diet, including plenty of livefood, is necessary throughout this period.

♦ RIGHT
A red-billed toucan shows the characteristic markings on its bill. It is virtually impossible to sex these birds visually, although hens may be slightly smaller than cocks. The bill itself is lightweight, with a honeycombed structure.

BREED BOX

Length	50 cm (20 in)
Incubation period	20 days
Fledging period	56 days
Clutch size	2–3 eggs

RED-BILLED HORNBILLS

Hornbills are sometimes regarded as the Old World equivalent of toucans, although their bills are not generally as highly coloured or as broad. The red-billed hornbill (*Tockus erythrorhynchus*) is the most widely kept member of the group, originating from Africa. Its small size, in comparison with other hornbills, makes it suitable for a garden aviary. In contrast to toucans, these hornbills are much quieter, with the male uttering a bubbling call when excited. Sexing is reasonably straightforward; the cocks have a swollen area, described as a casque, on the top of their bill.

Although primarily insectivorous by nature, these birds eat a range of foods, including low-iron mynah pellets, diced fruit which they swallow whole, and berries of various types.

The breeding habits of these birds are fascinating, and involve the hen being walled up inside the nest by her mate for some of the time, to protect her from predators such as snakes. Damp mud and clay should be provided for this purpose. The hen lays four or six eggs and ten weeks later, the young hornbills emerge. In the meantime, the male feeds his mate through a slit in the mud wall, although towards the end of the nesting period, when the young require more food, the hen may break outside to assist in feeding the brood.

For much of the remainder of the year, hornbills are very inactive, sitting with their heads hunched down on their shoulders. This is a normal posture and not a cause for concern. Although hardy, it is absolutely vital that hornbills are made to roost in a warm shelter when the temperature outside is set to fall below freezing, because these birds are prone to frost-bite, which will cause the loss of toes and can lead to difficulty in perching.

◆ LEFT
The speckled patterning over the wings is a feature of the red-billed hornbill and related species from Africa.

BREED BOX

Length	45 cm (18 in)
Incubation period	not applicable
Fledging period	70 days
Clutch size	4–6 eggs

◆ BELOW
The red-billed hornbill may appear to have eyelashes, but these are modified feathers rather than hairs. Cock birds have longer, bigger bills than hens.

RED-BILLED BLUE PIES

Many members of the crow family are predominantly black and white, but the red-billed blue pie (*Urocissa erythrorhyncha*) is a spectacular exception to the rule. It has cobalt-blue markings, while the bill, legs and feet are reddish in colour. The sexes are similar, although in most cases cock birds will have brownish irises.

BREED BOX	
Length	60 cm (24 in)
Incubation period	17 days
Fledging period	21 days
Clutch size	3–6 eggs

A pair of these corvids should be kept on their own in a spacious aviary. They need plenty of branches so they can hop from one to another, with uncluttered areas offering substantial flying space as well. Provide the birds with a large wicker basket, as commonly sold in garden centres for houseplants, for them to use as a nesting platform, and they will construct a loose assortment of twigs and sticks on top of it. The hen lays three to six eggs and these should hatch after about 17 days. For the first week or so, there is a real risk that the chicks may be cannibalized by the adult birds. This is more likely to occur if all the food is provided within easy reach. It is therefore a good idea

◆ ABOVE
The brilliant blue coloration of the red-billed blue pie may differ in depth between individuals. There is also a yellow-billed form that is less commonly seen in collections.

to scatter livefood around the flight to keep the adults actively searching for it. The young birds grow rapidly and are ready to leave the nest by three weeks of age. Once they are feeding independently, they should be transferred to separate quarters.

HARTLAUB'S TOURACOS

This distinctive group of African birds feeds largely on fruit, berries and greenstuff, which should be chopped into pieces. Chickweed, dandelions and cress, which can be grown very easily at home, are just some of the possible options. Sprinkle on a low-iron softbill food.

Cocks can be very spiteful towards intended partners, so it is better to start out with a genuine proven pair if

BREED BOX	
Length	40 cm (16 in)
Incubation period	21 days
Fledging period	28 days
Clutch size	2 eggs

possible. Hartlaub's touraco (*Tauraco hartlaubi*) is one of the most commonly bred species. It originates from parts of Tanzania and Kenya. A densely planted aviary reduces the likelihood of aggression during the breeding season, with touracos building a platform-type nest on a suitable support. The two eggs hatch after a period of three weeks, and the young fledge when they are about a month old.

Although hardy, touracos need adequate protection during periods of cold weather because they are susceptible to frostbite.

◆ LEFT
The red pigment in the flight feathers of Hartlaub's touraco is derived from a copper-based compound, and is unique in the animal kingdom. These birds are also unusual in not having a fixed perching grip, which means they can grip with three toes in front of the perch and one behind, or in a 2:2 configuration.

AUSTRALIAN
PARAKEETS

These parakeets were the first group of parrots to be bred successfully on a regular basis in aviary surroundings. It happened during the later years of the 1800s, before the requirements of such birds were well understood, which shows their adaptability. They are very easy to maintain on a diet of seed and greenstuff, although the best results are obtained by offering a wider range of foodstuffs. A mixture of millets and plain canary seed, augmented by a little sunflower seed and groats, will suffice for the smaller species, such as the grass parakeets. The percentage of thicker-shelled seeds, such as small pine nuts and safflower, should be increased for other members of the group.

Pairs should be housed separately from other birds. Never introduce a hen to a cock at the start of the breeding season because she may be attacked if she does not immediately respond to his advances. Pairs start to breed at the onset of spring. Provide a nest box lined with either wood shavings or softwood offcuts, which the larger species will be able to whittle away to form an absorbent nest lining. Visual sexing is possible in most cases. Most pairs of Australian parakeets are quite prolific, and will have two clutches of eggs in succession.

♦ OPPOSITE
The splendid grass parakeet, also called
the scarlet-chested because of the rich red
plumage evident on the cock's breast, is
an ideal choice for a garden aviary.

♦ LEFT
As the popularity of some parakeets
such as the splendid has grown, so colour
mutations have emerged in breeding stock.
This is a blue form of the species, with the
hen on the right.

BUDGERIGARS

The budgerigar (*Melopsittacus erithacus*) is the most popular pet bird in the world. These attractive Australian parakeets were first brought to Europe during the 1840s, and before the end of that century were being bred on a tremendous scale. Some breeding establishments in France housed as many as 100,000 birds.

Part of the reason for the budgerigar's popularity is its friendly nature, coupled with its powers of mimicry. These small parakeets rank among the champion chatterboxes of the avian world; some individuals are able to build up vocabularies of 500 words or more, which is far more than most members of the parrot family, with the exception of the African grey parrot. But whereas greys can be rather shy mimics, the budgerigar is quite willing, in most cases, to run through its repertoire in front of strangers.

Their calls are not loud and, unlike many parrots, budgerigars are not very destructive by nature, so they are quite easy to house in aviary surroundings, in flights made from 19 gauge mesh. Budgerigars are also quite hardy, and provided that they have a dry and well-lit shelter where they can retreat when the weather is bad, they do not require artificial heating or lighting.

One of the other major reasons underlying the popularity of the budgerigar is the range of colour varieties which have been developed. There are literally millions of possible combinations, taking into account the range of colours, markings and crested forms which now exist. This makes them popular exhibition birds and they are bred especially for that purpose. Budgerigars are judged by set standards and exhibition birds are significantly larger than their pet and aviary counterparts. Ordinary budgerigars will breed well when housed as a group, but their exhibition counterparts are usually separated in breeding cages, where the parentage of the chicks can be guaranteed.

If you are interested in exhibiting budgerigars, you must have a separate birdroom with space for breeding cages, and a training area for the birds prior to the show season. Heating and lighting will be needed because exhibition budgerigars are bred during the late winter in northern temperate areas.

The breeding period in aviaries is usually restricted to the warmer months of the year. Budgerigars are naturally prolific birds and in order to discourage them, nest boxes must be removed before winter. Hens breeding at this stage are particularly vulnerable to egg-binding, and the overall results are likely to be unsatisfactory.

◆ ABOVE
Light green and sky blue budgerigars. Both these birds are cocks, as shown by the blue ceres above the bill. Light green is the budgie's natural colour.

◆ ABOVE
Dark green recessive pied budgerigar cock. In this case, the cere is purplish, rather than blue. All three shades can be combined separately with the vibrant yellow plumage.

PET BUDGERIGARS

When it comes to choosing a budgerigar as a pet, it is the age of the bird rather than its coloration that is significant. Talking ability does not depend on variety, nor is it true that only cock birds will talk. Hens can be effective mimics but their natural calls are often slightly harsher in tone than the males'. The major drawback of having a hen as a pet is that she is likely to become very destructive at

◆ ABOVE
The albino hen budgerigar
is pure snow white in colour,
although birds can show a slight
blue suffusion in some lights.

COMMON FORMS OF BUDGERIGAR

Greens	These include the light green, which is the colour of the wild budgerigar. There are also dark greens and olive greens, created by the dark factor being superimposed on the light green colouring.
Blues	The sky blue is the lightest shade. The cobalt and mauve are the dark factor forms. The violet is also a member of this group, and is one of the most sought-after of all budgerigar colours, particularly the yellow-faced form. This local colour change can be combined with the other blue colours, as well as the grey mutation, to create equivalent yellow-faced varieties.
Pieds	There are two distinct forms of pied, which can be distinguished both visually and genetically. The Australian dominant pied is larger than its Danish recessive counterpart, and has black eyes with obvious irises, whereas the eyes of the Danish form are simply plum-coloured. The markings of pieds are variable, but the colour combinations are typically either yellow and green or white and blue.
Lutino and albino	These are pure yellow or white respectively, with red eyes.
Opaline	The heads are more lightly marked than normal, with a clear area forming a V-shape at the top of the wings.
Cinnamon	The wing markings are brownish rather than black.
Clearwings	The collective term used to describe the wing marking colours corresponding to (yellow wing) green and (whitewing or slightly darker greywing) blue series budgerigars.
Spangle	A mutation with pale centres to the feathers on the back and wings. Double factor spangles are of a decidedly paler shade than single factor birds.
Crests	These occur independently of colour. Three types are recognized – tufted, full-crested and half-crested forms.

certain times once she is mature and coming into breeding condition. It may not be just the sandsheet at the bottom of her cage which she rips up. Outside her quarters, the hen may strip wallpaper, or nibble at flaking paintwork, sometimes poisoning herself with fatal consequences.

Hens do not need to be paired up in order to lay eggs. If she does lay, do not remove the eggs because this will simply encourage her to produce more, just like a chicken. This will drain the hen's body reserves of calcium and other minerals, leaving her at greater risk of suffering from egg-binding, with the shell of the egg being rubbery rather than firm. Cock budgerigars, too, may develop behavioural difficulties when they come into breeding condition. This usually takes the form of regurgitating seed to a favoured toy or mirror. Such

BREED BOX

Length	20 cm (8 in)
Incubation period	18 days
Fledging period	35 days
Clutch size	4–6 eggs

◆ BELOW
The violet is highly sought-after because of its
colour. It is possible to create other varieties
involving this colour, such as violet pieds.

behaviour can be distinguished from the illness known as sour crop because the budgerigar constricts its pupils and appears very alert rather than off-colour. Even so, action needs to be taken to prevent weight loss; removing the object for two or three weeks should allow this phase to pass.

It is quite difficult to sex young budgerigars when they are between six and nine weeks old, which is the best time to obtain one as a pet. The cere of cock birds, i.e. the area above the bill encircling the nostrils, tends to be more prominent and of a deep purplish shade at this age, compared with hens. Once a young budgerigar starts to moult for the first time, at about 12 weeks old, sexing becomes

◆ ABOVE
The opaline mutation, seen here in combination with sky-blue, affects the budgerigar's body markings, rather than the coloration itself. It is sex-linked character in terms of its mode of inheritance.

much more straightforward because the cere shows its adult coloration. The cere colour of hens is always brown; that of cock birds is generally blue, although for the lutino, albino and recessive pied varieties it remains purple. The depth of brown coloration in hens varies through the year, becoming much darker at the start of the breeding season.

◆ ABOVE
Some budgerigar colour combinations can be complex, as shown by this golden face mauve spangle.

When selecting a budgerigar, there are a number of tell-tale indicators which can be used to confirm the bird's age. In the first place, in a young bird, the barring on the head, associated with most varieties, extends right down to the cere without an intervening area of clear plumage, which is why young birds are described as barheads. The spots on the face are generally less pronounced, while there is no white iris around the eyes, as seen in adult budgerigars of most varieties. There may also be a dark tip to the upper bill in chicks that have recently fledged.

Most young budgerigars are instinctively tame, and by placing your hand parallel with the perch, it should not be too difficult to persuade a fledgling to step on to your outstretched finger. Before finalizing your choice, however, ask to see the wings held open. Any missing flight feathers along the back edge may indicate the feather ailment French Moult, which is caused by a virus. Although in mild cases the feathers will regrow normally, in more severe cases the bird's ability to fly will be permanently handicapped.

AVIARY BIRDS

If you are seeking budgerigars for a colony aviary, you will need to obtain these prior to the start of the breeding season. The introduction of any birds after this time will be disruptive and can result in severe fighting between hens for possession of a nest box. Even in an established group, this can be a problem. It is essential to provide twice as many nest boxes as pairs, and position them so that they are all at the same height. Before the start of

the breeding season, ensure that there are the same number of cocks and hens in the aviary. Even so, budgerigars are promiscuous, and cocks will often mate with other hens once their own partner is incubating eggs on her own.

Although budgerigars are mature by six to nine months old, it is usual not to allow pairs to nest until they are at least a year old. Hens will then breed reliably until they are five or six, by which time their clutch size is likely to be declining, although cock

◆ ABOVE
Crested varieties of the budgerigars have also been developed. This is a full circular created grey cock bird. A crest can be combined with any variety.

◆ LEFT
Opaline grey-green dominant pied cock. This particular mutation is larger in size than the recessive pied and has more prominent cheek spots, as well as black eyes with white irises.

birds can remain fertile for most of their lives. Hens typically lay four to six eggs, which hatch after a period of 18 days. Young budgerigars fledge at about five weeks old, by which time the hen will have probably laid again. Pairs should be restricted to two clutches of chicks in succession. Budgerigars do not need nesting material; instead, they lay on wooden concaves, usually supplied with the nest box. It is useful to have a spare concave so that you can change these over when one becomes soiled, scrubbing off the used one and leaving it to dry.

When seeking breeding stock, it is impossible to age budgerigars once they have moulted into adult plumage unless they are fitted with a closed ring around one leg, engraved with the year in which they hatched; "00", for example, indicates a bird hatched in 2000. The only other possible clue may be the condition of the feet and legs. If these are heavily scaled, this is often indicative of an older bird.

When buying aviary stock, check the bill for signs of scaly face mites, which leave mini snail-like tracks in the first instance, before progressing to the characteristic coral-like encrustations at the sides of the bill. Similar signs may be evident on the legs as well. These parasites spread very rapidly in aviary surroundings, and are hard to eliminate. Treatment is quite straightforward, though, so if you want a particular budgerigar that is infected with these parasites, go ahead provided that you can keep the bird apart until it has fully recovered.

You should also check the bill to ensure that the upper and lower portions are properly aligned. This is an inherited weakness with no cure. The bill will have to be trimmed back regularly, so it is preferable not to buy such birds.

EXHIBITION STOCK

You are unlikely to find birds of exhibition quality at your local pet store. You will probably have to seek out an established exhibitor in order to obtain suitable birds. Such breeders can be tracked down in your neighbourhood through the national budgerigar organization in your country, or through the advertisement columns of the bird-keeping journals. Set yourself a budget and remember that it is better to buy a few birds of good quality than more birds of mediocre quality. Do not expect to purchase the best birds in the stud. Follow the breeder's advice – most are genuine and keen to help novices. It helps to specialize in a particular colour variety; most leading studs have acquired their reputations in specific areas because it is easier to concentrate on developing the required features associated with one single variety.

◆ ABOVE
In the case of the yellow-face cinnamon sky blue, the wing markings are transformed from black to a warm shade of brown. The throat spots are also brown.

◆ ABOVE
The rich buttercup yellow lutino and the snow-white albino are both red-eyed varieties due to the lack of the black pigment melanin in their bodies. Their feet are pink.

GRASS PARAKEETS

The grass parakeets are the most widely kept birds out of the entire group of Australian parakeets. Their relatively small size and characteristic quiet nature mean they are easy to accommodate even in a fairly small garden. They are quite hardy, although they can be vulnerable to intestinal roundworms. This is a reflection of the length of time they spend foraging for food on the floor of the flight; in this way they easily pick up the microscopic roundworm eggs. These are attractive birds and several stunning colour mutations have been established.

SPLENDID GRASS PARAKEETS

Some breeders consider the splendid grass parakeet (*Neophema splendida*) to be even more attractive than the turquoisine. The cock bird has a bright scarlet area on its chest, offset against the brilliant blue coloration of the head. Hens, in comparison, have green chests. The best-known mutation is the sea-green or dilute blue, in which the scarlet of the cock's breast is transformed to a salmon shade, with the green areas having a decidedly bluish hue. A pure blue form, with a white breast in the case of the cock, has also been established. Although hardy, these and other grass parakeets require a well-lit aviary shelter and may suffer respiratory problems during foggy weather.

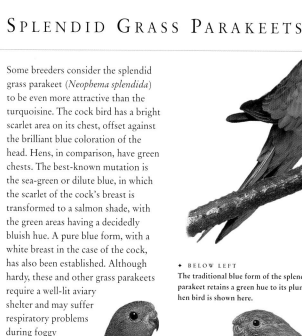

◆ LEFT
The splendid grass parakeet is so-called because of its striking appearance. Only the cock has the red feathering on the breast. This is a good choice for a garden aviary.

◆ BELOW LEFT
The traditional blue form of the splendid grass parakeet retains a green hue to its plumage. A hen bird is shown here.

◆ BELOW
The pure blue form of the splendid grass parakeet is less common than the greenish variant. The cock is shown on the left. Note the white and slight salmon coloration.

BREED BOX	
Length	20 cm (8 in)
Incubation period	19 days
Fledging period	30 days
Clutch size	5–6 eggs

TURQUOISINE GRASS PARAKEETS

◆ BELOW
This is an orange-bellied example of the turquoise grass parakeet, a cock bird as shown by the red areas on the wings. Mutations are widely available in this group of parakeets.

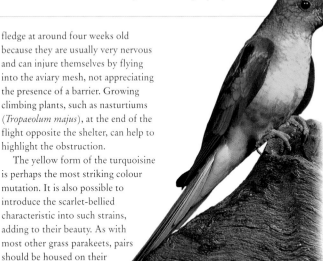

The turquoisine grass parakeet (*N. pulchella*) originates from the south-east of Australia. Sexing is straightforward with cocks having red patches on their wings.

The incubation period lasts approximately 19 days. Great care needs to be taken when the young fledge at around four weeks old because they are usually very nervous and can injure themselves by flying into the aviary mesh, not appreciating the presence of a barrier. Growing climbing plants, such as nasturtiums (*Tropaeolum majus*), at the end of the flight opposite the shelter, can help to highlight the obstruction.

The yellow form of the turquoisine is perhaps the most striking colour mutation. It is also possible to introduce the scarlet-bellied characteristic into such strains, adding to their beauty. As with most other grass parakeets, pairs should be housed on their own, rather than in groups.

BREED BOX	
Length	20 cm (8 in)
Incubation period	19 days
Fledging period	30 days
Clutch size	5–6 eggs

BOURKE'S PARAKEETS

Bourke's parakeet (*N. bourkii*) has one of the most distinctive colour schemes of all parrots. It is of a greyish-brown shade with pink underparts. This latter feature has been developed in the rosa form, which displays very strong pink coloration. Sexing is harder in this species than for other grass parakeets; hens tend to lack the blue frontal band seen on the heads of cocks, and have whiter heads as a result. Like other species, Bourke's parakeets are normally more active towards dusk than during the day.

BREED BOX	
Length	23 cm (9 in)
Incubation period	19 days
Fledging period	28 days
Clutch size	4–5 eggs

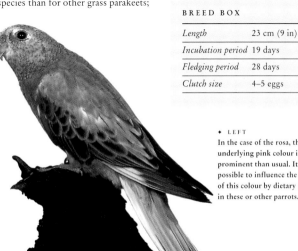

◆ LEFT
In the case of the rosa, the underlying pink colour is more prominent than usual. It is not possible to influence the depth of this colour by dietary means in these or other parrots.

◆ ABOVE
Bourke's parakeet has unusual coloration. These are active birds, like other grass parakeets, and are unsuitable as household pets, but they will thrive in aviary surroundings.

61

RED-RUMPED PARAKEETS

A popular Australian parakeet is the red-rumped (*Psephotus haematonotus*), which measures about 28 cm (11 in) long. Cocks can be easily sexed by their bright green colour; the hens are much greyer and lack the distinctive red feathering on the rump. It is better to purchase young birds if possible, rather than attempting to pair up adult birds. Some cocks can be very aggressive and may even kill their male chicks prior to fledging. Young birds hatched in the spring will breed during the following year.

Incubation lasts approximately 18 days, with the young fledging after four or five weeks in the nest. They should be removed as soon as they are feeding independently, by which time the adult pair is likely to be starting to nest again.

A number of mutations have been established, including blue and lutino forms and a pied.

✦ ABOVE
This is a pair of red-rumped parakeets. The hen is much the duller of the two. Pairs normally nest readily but watch for signs of aggression from the cock bird.

✦ LEFT
The lutino form of the red-rump is a relatively new mutation, being mainly pure yellow with red eyes.

BREED BOX

Length	28 cm (11 in)
Incubation period	18 days
Fledging period	32 days
Clutch size	4–6 eggs

✦ ABOVE
The yellow mutation of the red-rump is not as colourful as its name suggests. This is a cock bird, which is more colourful than a yellow red-rump hen.

BLUE BONNET PARAKEETS

The blue bonnet parakeet, or *P. haematogaster*, is less common than the red-rump, but requires similar care. The red patch on the cock's abdomen is usually larger and more richly coloured than in hens. These birds can be quite playful by nature, which is not a trait commonly associated with Australian parakeets.

BREED BOX

Length	28 cm (11 in)
Incubation period	21 days
Fledging period	37 days
Clutch size	4–5 eggs

✦ ABOVE
The unusual name of the blue bonnet comes from the blue feathering on the sides of its head.

ROSELLA PARAKEETS

Rosella parakeets may be identified without difficulty thanks to the scalloped markings on their backs, a feature unique to these birds. Unsurprisingly, the most colourful species are the most widely kept, such as the crimson rosella, also called Pennant's parakeet (*Platycercus elegans*). While adult birds are brick-red, the young are usually greenish in colour. Visual sexing in the case of rosellas is impossible; DNA sexing will be required.

The eastern (*P. eximius*) or golden-mantled rosella (GMR) is another widely bred species. These birds are prolific, with hens often laying six or seven eggs in a clutch and rearing all the chicks successfully. It takes approximately 26 days for the eggs to hatch, and the young parakeets leave the nest box when they are about five weeks old. On occasions, pairs may be double-brooded, and these parakeets can live for over 20 years.

✦ RIGHT
Pennant's parakeet is also known as the crimson rosella, thanks to the colour of its plumage. Prolific and hardy, these are popular aviary birds.

BREED BOX

Length 25–30 cm (10–12 in)	
Incubation period 26 days	
Fledging period	35 days
Clutch size	5–7 eggs

✦ BELOW
The blue mutation of Pennant's parakeet has become readily available over recent years.

✦ RIGHT
Eastern rosellas rank among the most colourful species, showing the characteristic scalloped markings which help to distinguish members of the rosella group.

BARNARD'S PARAKEETS

Barnard's parakeet (*Barnardius barnardi*) is a close relative of the rosellas, sharing with them the characteristic of tail feathers that do not taper along their length. This is why this group of Australian parakeets are known collectively as broadtails. They need the same care as other Australian parakeets, and an equally lengthy flight of at least 3.6 m (12 ft) with perches at either end, in view of their active nature. Sexing can be difficult; hens tend to have a greenish tinge to the blue mantle area on the back. Incubation of the four to six eggs lasts 19 days, with the young fledging about five weeks later.

BREED BOX	
Length	33 cm (13 in)
Incubation period	19 days
Fledging period	35 days
Clutch size	4–6 eggs

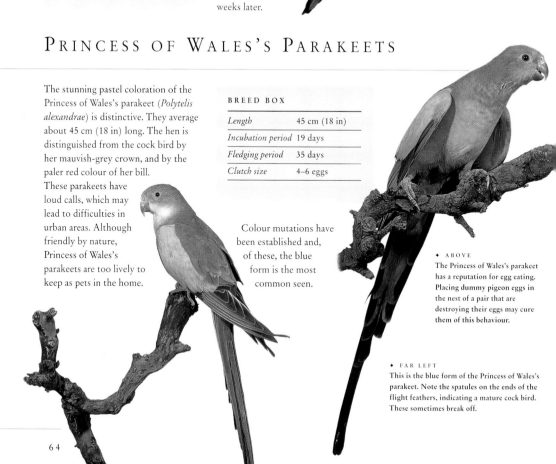

+ ABOVE
Barnard's parakeet is one of the less common Australian species in aviculture, although its care creates no special problems. It is a close relative of the rosellas.

PRINCESS OF WALES'S PARAKEETS

The stunning pastel coloration of the Princess of Wales's parakeet (*Polytelis alexandrae*) is distinctive. They average about 45 cm (18 in) long. The hen is distinguished from the cock bird by her mauvish-grey crown, and by the paler red colour of her bill. These parakeets have loud calls, which may lead to difficulties in urban areas. Although friendly by nature, Princess of Wales's parakeets are too lively to keep as pets in the home.

BREED BOX	
Length	45 cm (18 in)
Incubation period	19 days
Fledging period	35 days
Clutch size	4–6 eggs

Colour mutations have been established and, of these, the blue form is the most common seen.

+ ABOVE
The Princess of Wales's parakeet has a reputation for egg eating. Placing dummy pigeon eggs in the nest of a pair that are destroying their eggs may cure them of this behaviour.

+ FAR LEFT
This is the blue form of the Princess of Wales's parakeet. Note the spatules on the ends of the flight feathers, indicating a mature cock bird. These sometimes break off.

BARRABAND'S PARAKEETS

Barraband's parakeet (*Polytelis swainsonii*) is related to the Princess of Wales's parakeet and is about the same size. Sexing is easy as the cock birds display yellow plumage on the throat.

BREED BOX

Length	40 cm (16 in)
Incubation period	19 days
Fledging period	35 days
Clutch size	4–6 eggs

Hens lay four to six eggs in a clutch, often preferring a natural log, rather than a deep nest box. Young birds look similar to adult hens but cocks may be more colourful at this stage, and only young males will sing, starting at just a few months old. It will take two years for the young to attain maturity.

✦ RIGHT
Barraband's parakeet can be sexed very easily once the birds are mature, but sexing youngsters is much harder.

PILEATED PARAKEETS

The pileated parakeet (*Purpureicephalus spurius*) is unusually coloured, with deep mauve feathering on its chest. Hens are significantly duller in coloration. In south-western Australia, where these birds originate, they use their distinctive bills to extract the seeds of the eucalypt called marri, which features prominently in

BREED BOX

Length	35 cm (14 in)
Incubation period	19 days
Fledging period	35 days
Clutch size	4–6 eggs

✦ RIGHT
The long bill is a particular feature of the pileated parakeet: it is a reflection of its feeding habits.

their diet. They eat a regular seed in aviary surroundings, but with their powerful bills can be very destructive. They should be housed in a strong aviary, clad with 16 gauge mesh. When they fledge, young pileated parakeets are much smaller than the adult birds and are predominantly green in colour. Their underparts are a greyish shade of mauve, and there are only odd scattered red feathers on their heads and undertail coverts. They will moult into adult plumage from the age of about a year old. Some young pileated parakeets have been known to breed in their first year, before they have acquired their adult plumage. Regular deworming, as in the case of other Australian species, is recommended.

AUSTRALIAN KING PARAKEETS

The male Australian king parakeet (*Alisterus scapularis*) is stunningly attractive. The hen is comparatively subdued with more green plumage on the head and chest. These birds need a long flight and a deep nest box, or hollow log, equipped with a suitable

BREED BOX	
Length	43 cm (17 in)
Incubation period	21 days
Fledging period	56 days
Clutch size	4–5 eggs

ladder to ensure that they can move in and out. The box should be located in a secluded part of the aviary. The hen lays a clutch of four or five eggs, which should hatch after three weeks.

◆ ABOVE
This is a cock Australian king parakeet. A large aviary with plenty of flying space is needed for these birds, along with a deep nest box.

The young will fledge at about two months old. However, you must be patient because it can take Australian king parakeets a couple of years to settle in their quarters after a move, before going to nest.

CRIMSON-WING PARAKEETS

Male crimson-wing parakeets (*Aprosmictus erythropterus*) are, as the name suggests, crimson in colour. Hens are mainly dull green. It is better to start out with young birds because older cock birds may be aggressive towards their potential mates. Provide a deep nest box, or hollow log, with a ladder for ease of access. The hen lays a clutch of three or six eggs, which should hatch after three weeks. The young fledge at six weeks old.

BREED BOX	
Length	30 cm (12 in)
Incubation period	21 days
Fledging period	42 days
Clutch size	3–6 eggs

◆ BELOW
The characteristic wing coloration of the crimson-wing is clearly seen in this cock bird.

◆ RIGHT
Crimson-wings require a relatively deep nest box, with a secure ladder giving them easy access to the interior. The structure must be well supported in the aviary because of its weight.

RING-NECKS AND RELATED PARAKEETS

The 14 species in the psittaculid group are widely distributed across north Africa through the Middle East and across Asia to parts of China. Those which are confined to islands, such as the Blyth's Nicobar parakeet (*Psittacula caniceps*) and Layard's parakeet (*P. calthorpae*), are essentially unknown in bird-keeping circles, and the Mauritius or echo parakeet (*P. echo*) ranks among the rarest parrots in the world. Others have a long avicultural history, and are widely kept and bred.

The psittaculid parakeets range from about 30 cm (12 in) to 50 cm (20 in) in length, with their long and flamboyant tails typically accounting for half the measurement. Although the young birds invariably resemble the hens, the dark stripes extending down the face from the sides of the cock's bill mean that distinguishing the sex of the adult bird is straightforward, especially as there will often be differences in plumage between the male and female of a species.

RING-NECKED PARAKEETS

The ring-necked parakeet (*P. krameri*) has the distinction of being the most widely distributed species of parrot in the world today. The African type (*P. k. krameri*) was highly prized by the Romans. The birds were housed

BREED BOX

Length	38 cm (15 in)
Incubation period	24 days
Fledging period	49 days
Clutch size	4–5 eggs

in cages made of ivory and silver, and slaves made responsible just for their care. Previously, the ancient Greeks had fallen under the charm of the Indian type (*P. k. manillensis*). Distinguishing between these two types is quite easy; the African is slightly smaller in body and has a darker upper mandible with a black tip, rather than bright red as in the Indian. Also, the head of the African is a paler shade of green.

◆ ABOVE
The African ring-necked parakeet *(above)* differs from its Indian relative *(above right)* in its overall coloration.

◆ RIGHT
The coloration of the bill provides an obvious means of distinguishing between the African and Indian forms of the ring-necked parakeet.

◆ ABOVE
Sexing adult ring-necks is straightforward thanks to the collar of the cock bird, but it may take two years for this feature to become apparent in young birds.

Ring-necks are relatively hardy birds once established in their quarters, but they must have adequate protection from the cold because they can be vulnerable to frostbite. It is possible to keep two pairs together in a large aviary, but both pairs should be introduced at the same time. There is no strong pair bond between cock and hen, with very little direct contact being observed between them outside the breeding period.

LEFT
The blue form of the Indian ring-neck is widely kept, making it one of the most popular colour forms.

◆ RIGHT
The primrose is one of the rarer colours. This one is a hen. It can take two years or more for ring-necks to start breeding, so establishing new colours is inevitably a slow process.

This makes it feasible to swap partners, although persuading a young cock to mate with an older hen can be difficult; he may not be confident enough to take this step. Ring-necks often roost in nest boxes throughout the year, and in the northern hemisphere they are among the earliest birds to start nesting. In mild weather, hens may lay as early as February. To protect against a sudden cold snap, however, make the nest boxes from thick timber and site them in a sheltered part of the aviary.

For all psittaculid species, the nest box needs to be deep, with a ladder attached inside, below the entrance hole, to give access to the base. Line the box with wood shavings and pieces of softwood battening that the birds can whittle away to make a nest lining.

Colour mutations have become widely established in the Indian type over recent years, and some of these are highly valued in India. They include the lutino form, in which the green plumage is replaced by yellow, and the cock's black facial feathering by white. The pinkish area encircling the neck is retained, appearing more prominent against the yellow plumage,

while the red upper bill is unaffected. The elegant blue mutation is very popular. The pink of the cock's collar has become modified to white, while the bill retains its red coloration. Hens are pure blue rather than green. Breeders have combined these colours to create a pure white albino with red eyes; the cocks have no collar. Other colour variants include pied, cinnamon and dark factor forms, as well as grey and grey-green. With mutation ring-necks, DNA testing enables those birds that are important for the future of the breeding programme to be identified at an early stage.

ALEXANDRINE PARAKEETS

The Alexandrine (*P. eupatria*) is closely related to the ring-necked parakeet, but is slightly larger with a more powerful bill. Alexandrines tend to nest later in the year than ring-necks, with hens laying clutches of two or three eggs. It takes up to three years for young cock birds to moult into adult plumage, but thanks to DNA techniques, it is possible to

distinguish the sexes well before this stage. With the Alexandrine, it can be very difficult to distinguish between genuine colour mutations and those created by hybridization with ring-necks. Hybrid birds are identifiable by their small size, when compared with true Alexandrine mutations, except in the case of the blue, where the red on the wings is replaced by white.

BREED BOX	
Length	50 cm (20 in)
Incubation period	28 days
Fledging period	49 days
Clutch size	2–3 eggs

◆ ABOVE AND LEFT
The Alexandrine parakeet makes an impressive aviary occupant, although pairs can be destructive. The hen bird lacks the neck collar.

DERBYAN PARAKEETS

The largest member of the psittaculid group is the Derbyan parakeet (*P. derbiana*), which is known to originate from the Himalayan region, ranging from north-east Assam through to south-eastern Tibet. The cock bird is particularly striking and easy to identify, thanks to the deep mauve shade of the underparts offset against the greenish wings, and orangish-red upper bill. Hens have black bills. These attractive parakeets are very hardy, but their loud calls and destructive nature mean that housing them satisfactorily may well be impossible in some locations.

Derbyans breed later than other psittaculid parakeets, perhaps because they originate from what can be a bitterly cold part of the world. Hens rarely lay before early summer in northern temperate areas. A typical clutch has two or three eggs and incubation takes about 26 days. The young leave the nest after about seven weeks. Increased amounts of roughage and fruit, as well as soaked seed, should be offered when they are rearing their chicks. Derbyans often show a particular fondness for pine nuts as part of their seed mix; these form part of their natural diet in the wild.

BREED BOX	
Length	50 cm (20 in)
Incubation period	26 days
Fledging period	49 days
Clutch size	2–3 eggs

◆ ABOVE
The Derbyan is the largest member of the group, and needs suitably robust accommodation. The cock bird is the more colourful of the pair.

MOUSTACHED PARAKEETS

The moustached parakeet (*P. alexandri*) is found over a wide area of south-east Asia. Sexes can be identified by bill colour – the hen's bill is black. There are a number of distinct types. In the Javan (*P. a. alexandri*), the hen has a pinkish bill, and pale pink breast feathering. Measuring approximately 33 cm (13 in) long, these parakeets have never been especially popular, possibly because they are rather noisy. They can also be quite destructive.

BREED BOX	
Length	33 cm (13 in)
Incubation period	23 days
Fledging period	50 days
Clutch size	3–4 eggs

◆ RIGHT
This pair of moustached parakeets show the broad black stripe around the bill, the reason for the common name of these parakeets.

LONG-TAILED PARAKEETS

In contrast with other members of the group, the long-tailed parakeet (*P. longicauda*) is not hardy, requiring very careful acclimatization and protection from frostbite on cold winter nights. The cock birds' narrow, elongated tail feathers measure up to 20 cm (8 in) long. Hens have brown rather than red bills, and a green rather than a black stripe extending back on the sides of the head. Mealworms may be eaten avidly as a rearing food.

BREED BOX	
Length	40 cm (16 in)
Incubation period	26 days
Fledging period	55 days
Clutch size	2–5 eggs

♦ RIGHT
Long-tailed parakeets are not as hardy as other members of the psittaculid group, and this must be reflected in their accommodation.

PLUM-HEADED PARAKEETS

The plum-headed parakeet (*P. cyanocephala*) is one of the most popular members of the group, probably due to its quiet nature, and soft, relatively musical calls. Averaging 35 cm (14 in) long, these parakeets are also very docile, even when breeding, and they can be housed in a spacious flight in the company of non-aggressive softbills or finches.

Although the sex of adult birds can be distinguished at a glance (by head colour), young cock birds with their grey heads resemble adult hens in appearance. Close inspection may reveal odd plum-coloured

BREED BOX	
Length	35 cm (14 in)
Incubation period	23 days
Fledging period	43 days
Clutch size	4–6 eggs

feathers, but obtaining a true pair of plum-heads can sometimes prove to be difficult.

Pairs nest readily, but in northern temperate areas it is a good idea to discourage them from breeding until April by withholding the nest box. This increases the likelihood of success. Hen plum-heads usually stop brooding their offspring – which can number up to six – before they are fully feathered, and this can lead to losses if there is a sudden cold snap. Even if this happens, or indeed their eggs fail to hatch, plum-heads are unlikely to show any interest in breeding again until the following year, and will abandon the nest box.

♦ LEFT
The plum-headed parakeet is an ideal choice for a garden aviary. Quiet, colourful and graceful in flight, these birds are justifiably popular.

CONURES AND RELATED PARAKEETS

"Conure" is the name given to some parakeets found in Central and South America that were formerly classified as *Conurus*. There are two major groupings, the aratinga conures, which make up the numerically bigger group, and the pyrrhura conures. Pyrrhuras are known as scaly-breasted conures because of the markings on their chest; aratingas are characteristically noisy and destructive.

Feeding conures is straightforward. A complete diet will prevent dietary deficiencies that could compromise breeding activities, but successful breeding is also possible on a seed-based diet, augmented by a supplement, plus vegetables and fruit. Millets, canary seed, groats, flaked maize, sunflower, safflower, pine nuts and hemp in restricted quantities should feature in the seed mixture.

BLUE-CROWNED CONURES

◆ BELOW
The blue-crowned conure is one of the larger *Aratinga* species, averaging 35cm (14in) long, with a powerful bill and loud voice.

The blue-crowned conure (*Aratinga acuticaudata*) occurs over a huge area of South America, from eastern Colombia in the north, southwards to parts of Paraguay, Uruguay and Argentina. It can be instantly identified by its coloration, with blue feathering apparent on the head, offset against the prominent white patch of skin encircling each eye. The remainder of the plumage is greenish, apart from the undersides of the tail feathers which have a reddish hue. Young birds have less blue on their heads, where it is restricted to the forehead and the crown. They can develop into affectionate, personable pets if obtained at an early age, although their talking abilities are rather limited.

BREED BOX

Length	35 cm (14 in)
Incubation period	26 days
Fledging period	52 days
Clutch size	3–4 eggs

WHITE-EYED CONURES

◆ LEFT
The bare white skin around the eyes accounts for the name of the white-eyed conure, although this particular feature is associated with a number of other species as well.

The white-eyed conure (*A. leucophthalmus*) is widely distributed across South America. Individual markings are a feature of the aratingas, and this is exemplified by the white-eyes. These birds are mainly green in colour, with red plumage evident along the leading edge of the wings. Scattered red feathers on the sides of the face and the head enable birds to be recognized. It is not true to say that cocks are more brightly coloured than hens. Young white-eyed conures have a duller coloration, having yellow rather than red wing markings.

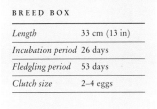

BREED BOX

Length	33 cm (13 in)
Incubation period	26 days
Fledgling period	53 days
Clutch size	2–4 eggs

Nest boxes must be provided throughout the year for roosting. The nest box should be about 30 cm (12 in) square and 45 cm (18 in) in depth. These conures are not especially popular in bird-keeping circles, probably because of their rather subdued coloration.

GOLDEN-CROWNED CONURES

The golden-crowned or peach-fronted conure (*A. aurea*) is found in the southern part of South America, ranging from Brazil to parts of Bolivia, Paraguay and Argentina. Although it measures just 25 cm (10 in) in length, it has a loud call, particularly if it is

BREED BOX

Length	25 cm (10 in)
Incubation period	26 days
Fledging period	50 days
Clutch size	3–4 eggs

disturbed for any reason, and its bill is powerful enough to inflict damage on any exposed, easily accessible timber in the aviary. There is a tendency for people to believe that the more colourful individuals are cock birds, but this is not borne out by DNA sexing.

Young peach-fronted conures have pale rather than black bills on fledging, with an area of yellow feathering immediately above the cere merging into orange.

A whitish upper bill is the feature of Petz's or the orange-fronted conure (*A. canicularis*), a Central American

♦ ABOVE
Immature golden-crowned conures are duller in colour than these adults, and it will take between two and three years for them to reach maturity.

species that can be confused with the golden-crowned, although the two species are widely separated in terms of their distribution.

SUN CONURES

The dazzling sun conure (*A. solistalis*) aroused tremendous interest in the early 1970s when breeding stock became available for the first time. Since then, they have become well established in aviculture. In the wild, they are generally to be found north of the Amazon, on the eastern side of South America, extending from Venezuela to Brazil.

BREED BOX

Length	30 cm (12 in)
Incubation period	26 days
Fledging period	50 days
Clutch size	3–4 eggs

Sun conures measure about 30 cm (12 in) long. They have proved to be hardy birds but their calls can be disturbing. This is their major drawback and likely to preclude them from being kept on a colony basis, as they are in some public collections. Sun conures can look particularly

♦ LEFT
When they fledge, sun conures have greenish backs and a greenish tone to their underparts. Their distinctive coloration takes two years to develop over successive moults.

spectacular as a breeding flock. The diversity in markings between individuals is clearly apparent; some are of a much more fiery shade than others, with a decidedly orange hue over much of their plumage. This does not appear to be an inherited characteristic, and both predominantly yellow and orange coloured chicks can occur in the same nest.

Young sun conures can develop into superb pets, and may be taught to whistle and repeat a few words. In the home, however, it is important to spray them regularly because otherwise they may be prone to feather-plucking, which can be a difficult habit to break. Toys and branches to gnaw will help to keep them occupied, and so prevent them from plucking their feathers out of boredom. Sun conures have a life expectancy of over 20 years.

FIERY-SHOULDERED CONURES

The chest markings of the fiery-shouldered conure (*Pyrrhura egregia*) are not especially prominent, and neither are the brown ear coverts, but the bare white skin encircling the eye is clearly evident, as is the fiery orange colour in the shoulder area on the wings. Young birds are not as brightly coloured as adults; their wing markings are less prominent.

Most pyrrhuras nest readily in aviary surroundings, if conditions are suitable. The successful establishment of the fiery-shouldered conure in barely a decade is proof of that. They will even breed successfully in indoor flights, provided that they have

adequate seclusion. Hens lay four or five eggs in a clutch, and incubation lasts 23 days. The young fledge at about seven weeks old. They should be transferred to separate accommodation as soon as they are feeding independently.

BREED BOX	
Length	25 cm (10 in)
Incubation period	23 days
Fledging period	51 days
Clutch size	4–5 eggs

♦ ABOVE
The fiery-shouldered conure is a relative newcomer on the avicultural scene. It was totally unknown in collections until 1988, but is now quite widely kept and bred.

SLENDER-BILLED CONURES

The unusual slender-billed conure (*Enicognathus leptorhynchus*) occurs in the wild at the tip of South America, in Chile. It resembles other members of the pyrrhura group both in the barring on its underparts and in overall coloration. However, it is significantly larger, measuring approximately 40 cm (16 in) overall, and instantly recognizable by its long, thin upper bill, which protrudes some distance over the lower mandible, and from which it takes its name.

BREED BOX	
Length	40 cm (16 in)
Incubation period	26 days
Fledging period	49 days
Clutch size	4–6 eggs

Virtually unknown in aviculture until the mid-1970s, pairs have proved to be good nesters, with the result that stock of this species is readily available. Young birds can become great companions, especially if hand-reared. Hens lay four to six eggs, and incubation lasts for 26 days. The young birds fledge at about seven weeks old. Hard-boiled egg is a popular rearing food, along with assorted greenstuff and soaked seed.

Aviaries for these conures should incorporate an area of grass, where the birds can dig for food using their bills, which are an adaptation to help them find food in their rather harsh native habitat. Even young slender-billed conures will very nearly have full-grown bills when they leave the nest. Young birds are best identified by the bare skin around their eyes, which is white in colour, rather than grey.

♦ ABOVE
Slender-billed conures use their distinctive elongated bills to dig for corms and roots. They should be housed in aviaries that incorporate an area of lawn for this reason.

BROTOGERIS PARAKEETS

The brotogeris group of parakeets occurs in parts of Central and South America. They average about 23 cm (9 in) in length, and are highly social birds, with breeding results most likely to be obtained when they are housed in small groups rather than as individual pairs. These parakeets can be quarrelsome, however, so it is important to have only sexed pairs and to introduce all members of the group to their aviary at the same time. Provide more nest boxes than pairs. Reintroducing any individuals that have been removed will be fraught with difficulty, although young birds that have been bred in the aviary will normally be accepted without problems. Brotogeris parakeets can be fed the same as conures, although fruit should form a more significant part of their diet.

CANARY-WINGED PARAKEETS

The canary-winged parakeet (*Brotogeris versicolurus chiriri*) is the most widely kept member of the brotogeris group. These birds are hardy once properly acclimatized, usually preferring to roost in a nest box rather than on a perch. The bright canary-yellow feathering on the edges of the wings, and the lime-green body colour distinguish it from the closely related white-winged parakeet (*B.v. versicolurus*), which is a darker shade of green. As with other brotogeris parakeets, there is no means of distinguishing the sexes by sight. Also, do not assume that two birds which preen each other are a true pair as this is not necessarily the case.

BREED BOX

Length	23 cm (9 in)
Incubation period	26 days
Fledging period	45 days
Clutch size	4–5 eggs

◆ ABOVE
In spite of their relatively small size, canary-winged parakeets are likely to prove destructive in aviary surroundings and may also be very noisy on occasions.

TOVI PARAKEETS

The tovi parakeet (*B. jugularis*) is also known as the orange-chinned parakeet. It is otherwise mainly green, aside from the bronzy brown plumage on the wings. While adult birds can be shy, young birds will develop into friendly pets. Hens lay between four and six eggs in a clutch and incubation lasts about 26 days. The chicks leave the nest at about six weeks old. Soaked seed and plenty of fruit should be offered regularly, particularly when pairs are breeding. These small parakeets are quite hardy once acclimatized.

BREED BOX

Length	17.5 cm (7 in)
Incubation period	26 days
Fledging period	42 days
Clutch size	4–6 eggs

◆ RIGHT
The highly social nature of brotogeris parakeets in general is shown by these tovis. Within colonies, however, strong pair bonds usually exist between individual members.

LINEOLATED PARAKEETS

The lineolated parakeet (*Bolborhynchus lineola*) has a wide distribution across much of Central America extending into northern South America. Its small size – it averages little more than 15 cm (6 in) in length – and quiet, gentle nature have led to the lineolated becoming very popular over recent years. This popularity has increased still further, thanks to the development of various colour mutations, including blue, lutino and dark factor variants.

BREED BOX	
Length	15 cm (6 in)
Incubation period	18 days
Fledging period	35 days
Clutch size	4–5 eggs

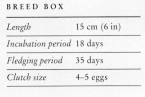

Pairs of these parakeets may sometimes be persuaded to breed in a spacious double budgerigar breeding cage, lined with coarse wood shavings, although results are likely to be better if they are housed in a flight. Hens lay four or five eggs, which hatch after 18 days. The young leave the nest at five weeks old.

♦ ABOVE
The lineolated parakeet is also known as the barred parakeet because of the variable black coloration on its plumage. Although cock birds are sometimes more heavily barred than hens, this is not always the case.

A diet of smaller seeds, such as millets, augmented with fresh foods suits these parakeets very well. Soft food may also be eaten, and is especially useful for breeding birds.

♦ ABOVE
The blue mutation of the lineolated parakeet is well established, with the black barring being retained.

MONK PARAKEETS

Although colour mutations are generally scarce among New World parakeets, they do occur with monk or quaker parakeets (*Myiopsitta monachus*). Blue and yellow colour mutations have been recorded. These parakeets are also unusual in that they use their nest for roosting. It is possible to allow them to build their nest if you can provide a raised platform and a supply of twigs from apple and sycamore trees. Colonies of birds may amass huge structures. In an aviary, the pair may breed in nest boxes. These birds nest more readily when housed in groups, due to their highly social nature: bear this in mind when planning a breeding programme.

BREED BOX	
Length	28 cm (11 in)
Incubation period	26 days
Fledging period	45 days
Clutch size	5–7 eggs

♦ ABOVE
The grey-breasted parakeet is another name for the monk or quaker parakeet. These birds must be housed in flights covered in 16 gauge mesh.

COCKATIELS

With their crests, and in their breeding behaviour, cockatiels
(*Nymphicus hollandicus*) resemble cockatoos, but they also have
a number of characteristics that are more typically associated
with Australian parakeets, and these have helped to ensure their
widespread popularity as aviary birds. For many years, the cockatiel
was overshadowed by its better-known Australian relative, the
budgerigar, but during the later years of the 20th century it achieved
worldwide popularity in its own right, thanks particularly
to the emergence of colour mutations.

♦ OPPOSITE
The red-eyed silver is one of the less
common mutations, shown here in the
company of a white-faced cock bird.

♦ ABOVE LEFT
The white-faced cockatiel cock bird
has a pure white face. The hen's facial
plumage is greyish.

COCKATIELS

The original grey form of the cockatiel is easy to recognize – predominantly grey with white patches on the wings. Cock birds have prominent yellow areas on the sides of their faces, with circular orange patches of plumage there as well. Adult hens are less distinctive. Their facial plumage is greyer, although the undersurface of their tail feathers is clearly barred with yellow.

Cockatiels are popular both as pets and aviary birds, but it is important to start out with a genuine youngster if you are seeking a companion bird. If possible, start off with a hand-raised chick. Recently fledged chicks resemble hens, although it is possible to identify them by

the pinkish tinge to the cere above the bill, incorporating the nostrils. Young birds' tail feathers are shorter than adults' when they are weaned and ready to be rehomed.

Young cockatiels can be nervous to start with, but they settle down quickly and will become very tame. Many people prefer cock birds as pets because of their attractive whistling calls, but unless the young cockatiels are sexed by means of DNA, it is impossible to distinguish the sexes until the cocks start singing at around three months of age. Cockatiels can live well into their teens, and have been known to live into their late twenties in some more exceptional cases.

Although cockatiels have a similar history of domestication to the budgerigar, becoming well known and widely bred from the 1840s onwards, it was not until a century later that the first mutation – the pied – became established. Pieds have variable areas of light and dark plumage, and the pattern of distribution is random and highly individual. Those having

extensive solid areas of colour are often described as lightly variegated.

It was the emergence of the lutino mutation in Florida during the late 1950s that first focused attention on the cockatiel. These birds are a striking pale lemon shade all over, with orange cheek patches. Visual sexing is still possible but harder than with the grey: the barring under the hen's tail feathers is not clearly defined against the white background.

BREED BOX	
Length	30 cm (12 in)
Incubation period	19 days
Fledging period	35 days
Clutch size	5–6 eggs

Feather-plucking is known to be a problem with various strains of lutino cockatiels: signs include having a slightly bald area behind the crest. If buying a new cockatiel, it helps to start out with young birds because you can be certain that they have not been feather-plucked. Nothing can be done once the feathers have been removed, other than waiting for them to grow back again. Take particular care with the housing of recently fledged cockatiels in this condition if the climate is anything but warm, because they are vulnerable to being chilled until their plumage has regrown.

Another highly attractive cockatiel mutation is the cinnamon, in which the grey plumage has become brownish. The cocks are a darker shade of brown than the hens, and the mutation is sex-linked in its mode of inheritance, the same as the lutino.

◆ ABOVE
Grey is the usual colour of cockatiels, as shown by this pair. Cockatiels breed well in aviaries, while young birds can develop into excellent companions.

◆ RIGHT
Sexing cockatiels is quite straight-forward. The cock bird's head is predominantly yellow, while the hen's is much greyer.

◆ **BELOW**
It is possible to combine the cinnamon characteristic with other mutations, as shown by this primrose cinnamon pied. In this case, the pied areas have a fairly pronounced yellow tone.

◆ **ABOVE**
The albino is pure white in colour and may be slightly smaller than normals. There is no variation in the plumage of male and female and so observing behavioural differences, such as the cock's song, is the only way to distinguish between them.

An unusual colour change occurred in Germany with the emergence of the pearl mutation. The centres of the individual feathers have lost pigment, and are thus paler than the edges. In the cock birds, this feature tends to become obscured with maturity. The pearl mutation is not linked with a particular colour and so can be seen in association with other forms as well, although it is less distinctive in the case of lutinos.

The emergence of the white-faced mutation is particularly significant. All yellow and orange pigmentation has disappeared from the feathering. As a result, cocks can be distinguished by their pure white heads; the hens' heads are greyish-white. By combining this mutation and the lutino, it has been possible to create the albino, which is pure white in colour with reddish eyes.

The silver mutations of the cockatiel occur in two forms, a dominant version which is fairly common, and a rare recessive form, with red eyes.

Recent mutations have resulted in changes to the ear patches, but these are not common.

With so many different mutations and varieties, it is not surprising that there is growing interest in exhibiting cockatiels, particularly in North America, where judging standards are well established.

Cockatiels are very easy to look after. Feed them on a budgerigar seed mix, augmented by some sunflower and safflower seeds, groats and a little hemp. Alternatively, offer a complete diet. If you are using seed, add a supplement to combat Vitamin A deficiency, which can contribute to chick mortality in the nest. Offer greenfood, apple and soft food regularly, particularly during the breeding period.

One of the less obvious charms of the cockatiel is its very gentle nature. Cockatiels can be kept with finches, quails, doves and non-aggressive softbills, although their size in a small flight can be upsetting to very small birds. You can also keep cockatiels on a colony basis, although breeding results are never as good as when they are housed in individual pairs. This is because they will share nest boxes, and the number of eggs laid is too great for a single bird to brood, increasing the likelihood of fatal chilling.

Both parents share incubation and brooding duties. As they grow older, the chicks hiss menacingly in the nest when they are disturbed. Pairs should be restricted to rearing two broods in a season. Remove the nest box in the autumn or they may attempt to breed right through the winter.

◆ **LEFT**
The markings of pied cockatiels are highly individual and not just in the feathering. In this individual, some dark pigment is retained on the bill. The feet, too, can be variable in colour.

◆ **ABOVE**
In the case of the cinnamon mutation, the grey colour assumes a brownish hue. This is a sex-linked mutation.

COCKATOOS

Cockatoos are among the most distinctive parrots, thanks to their crests, which they will raise when excited or alarmed. They originate from islands off the coasts of Indonesia and New Guinea, and their distribution extends to Australia. The group can be broadly divided into two categories – the black cockatoos and those with predominantly white feathering. The black are rare in aviculture compared with the white.

One of the greatest difficulties is in ensuring compatibility between the members of a pair. It is not uncommon for a pair to live in harmony until the start of the breeding season, when the cock will turn on his mate, seriously attacking or even killing her. Even a proven pair can offer no guarantee. Starting out with odd birds is especially dangerous, particularly if the hen is younger than her mate and nesting for the first time. The safest option is to acquire young birds, having had them sexed by the DNA method, and then wait for them to breed in due course. Having grown up together, the bond between them is likely to be greater than when two adult birds are put together. Once established, pairs of cockatoos may breed successfully for more than 20 years.

◆ OPPOSITE
Strikingly attractive, but expensive and problematic to pair up successfully, the Major Mitchell's or Leadbeater's cockatoo is only suitable for experienced breeders.

◆ LEFT
When resting, cockatoos like this citron-crested keep their crest feathers folded back over the top of the head. The shape of the crest varies between the members of this group.

LESSER SULPHUR-CRESTED COCKATOOS

The lesser sulphur-crested cockatoo (*Cacatua sulphurea*) is commonly kept as a pet and for breeding, and is recognized by its yellow ear patches and crest. Another popular choice is the citron-crested (*C. s. citrinocristata*), with its distinctive orange plumage.

Cockatoos are not an ideal choice for the novice bird-keeper because of their temperament. They will screech for long periods and can be destructive; they need well-built accommodation and no neighbours. Their behaviour may worsen as they grow older, particularly if hand-reared, because they then have no instinctive fear of people, and will bite readily.

BREED BOX

Length	30 cm (12 in)
Incubation period	28 days
Fledging period	75 days
Clutch size	2 eggs

♦ LEFT
A lesser sulphur-crested cockatoo reveals the beauty of its crest feathering. The greater sulphur-crested is not only significantly larger but also has far less distinct yellow patches on the sides of the head.

♦ ABOVE
The citron-crested subspecies of the lesser sulphur-crested cockatoo can be easily identified by the orange rather than yellow areas of plumage.

UMBRELLA COCKATOOS

The largest of the white cockatoos is the umbrella (*C. alba*), so-called because of the shape of its broad crest. It measures 48 cm (19 in) in length, and originates from the northern and central Moluccan Islands of Indonesia.

BREED BOX

Length	48 cm (19 in)
Incubation period	28 days
Fledging period	84 days
Clutch size	2 eggs

Sexing is carried out visually: the hen's iris is red-brown, whereas that of the cock is usually black. Young birds can be identified by the grey colour of their eyes. Male and female birds share the incubation of a clutch of two eggs. If both eggs hatch, a size difference will develop as one assumes dominance and takes more of the food. The weaker chick will need to be hand-reared if it is to survive.

♦ RIGHT
The broad crest feathers that help to distinguish the umbrella cockatoo, along with its white plumage, can be clearly seen here.

DUCORP'S COCKATOOS

In recent years, a small number of the attractive Ducorp's cockatoo (*C. ducorpsi*) from the Solomon Islands have become available to bird-keepers. These birds are beginning to breed and are becoming established in overseas collections. They average about 30 cm (12 in) in length, have a relatively short crest, and blue skin around the eyes. Unlike many cockatoos, they can be persuaded to sample greenstuff, fruit and vegetables quite readily, particularly when they are rearing chicks.

BREED BOX	
Length	30 cm (12 in)
Incubation period	25 days
Fledging period	62 days
Clutch size	2 eggs

✦ RIGHT
Ducorp's cockatoo has a relatively small crest and a blue area of skin surrounding the eyes.

GALAH COCKATOOS

The galah or roseate cockatoo (*Eolophus roseicapillus*) is one of the easier species to manage, although over-reliance on sunflower seed in the diet can cause problems, giving rise to lipomas (fatty tumours). It can be difficult to persuade cockatoos to alter their dietary preferences, so always offer them a varied diet from the outset. Try a complete diet, which offers a more nutritionally balanced alternative to seed alone.

The pink and grey colour scheme of the galah cockatoo is unique. These birds may mature as early as two years old and are more prolific than the white cockatoos, sometimes laying four or five eggs. Incubation is shared in typical cockatoo fashion. Compatability between members of the pair is far less a problem in the case of these cockatoos, compared to their *Cacatua* cousins. Occasional colour variants have also been recorded, noticeably a white-backed form where grey plumage is replaced by white feathering. As with other cockatoos, galahs are hardy when housed in aviaries, while, temperamentally, they make better pets than other species. No cockatoos are especially talented as talking birds, although they can learn to whistle a passable tune.

BREED BOX	
Length	35 cm (14 in)
Incubation period	25 days
Fledging period	49 days
Clutch size	2–5 eggs

✦ RIGHT
The galah cockatoo is one of the more dependable species of cockatoo for breeding, although much depends on the individual temperaments of a pair.

LORIES AND LORIKEETS

These colourful parrots originate from islands off the coast of Indonesia, New Guinea, the Pacific Islands and Australia. Many display areas of bright red in their plumage and their striking coloration is part of the appeal of this group of birds, quite apart from their friendly personalities.

Lories and lorikeets differ from other parrots in their feeding habits. They rely heavily on flowers for the nectar and pollen, which is the mainstay of their diet, although they will also eat fruit and roughage. In the past, keepers were forced to rely on their own recipes, which were not always nutritionally sound, but today, excellent commercial brands are available in powdered form to be mixed with water. Read the instructions carefully and do not mix up more nectar than will be required for one day, as any that is not consumed must be discarded before it sours. It is important to clean out the drinker thoroughly, using a bottle brush and washing up liquid to remove any trace of old residues. Never provide nectar in open containers because the birds will try to bathe in them. For those housed inside, provide a separate container of water for bathing.

Dry lory diets are available, which can be offered separately or sprinkled over fruit. Few breeders use them exclusively in place of a nectar solution, although they do add variety to the diet when used in moderation.

◆ OPPOSITE
Various lories and lorikeets like these Musschenbroek's are small, quiet birds. They are easy to accommodate in aviary surroundings.

◆ LEFT
Active, lively and inquisitive by nature, lories like the black-winged make personable aviary occupants, often becoming very tame with their keepers.

LORIES AND LORIKEETS

Feeding lories is not especially difficult in most cases because their lively, curious natures ensure that they are usually quite willing to sample unfamiliar items in their food dish with little hesitation. This means that you can take advantage of fruits in season, but offer only small quantities at first, increasing the amount gradually, so as to avoid changing the birds' diet suddenly. Especially when first acquired, they can be vulnerable to enterotoxaemia, a bacterial illness which is likely to be rapidly fatal.

The liquid droppings of this group of birds means that they are not popular as pets, being messy in the home, but they do make very lively companions and can master a few words. In aviary surroundings, their accommodation needs to take account of their diet. Easily washable surfaces should feature on the walls of the shelter, while it helps if the floor of the flight is of paving slabs or concrete which can also be washed off easily. Visual sexing is not possible.

GREEN-NAPED LORIKEETS

The green-naped lorikeet (*Trichoglossus haematodus*) is one of the most widely distributed lorikeets, occurring in more than 20 different forms across its wide range, which extends from parts of Asia to southern Australia. Dark green wings, a colourful breast, bluish head feathering and a contrasting green area on the sides of the head is the typical coloration of green-naped lorikeets.

Pairs will usually nest quite readily. It is sensible to line the nest box with a thick layer of wood shavings, in view of the liquid nature of their diet. The incubation period lasts for 27 days, with the chicks fledging at about eight weeks old. This stage can be identified by the fledglings' dark irises and bills.

Feather-plucking of the chicks can be a problem with some pairs; often the problem will be resolved only when the chicks leave the nest. The damaged plumage will regrow but there is a danger that the young birds will behave in the same way towards their own offspring.

Green-naped lorikeets will live happily enough in a colony in a large aviary, where they make an entertaining sight, although they can be noisy. Have the birds sexed first, and space the nest boxes around the flight at the same height to prevent any squabbling. Providing a choice of nest boxes is also important to breeding success.

♦ LEFT
Green-naped lorikeets have patches of greenish-yellow plumage on the nape of the neck, and darker edging to the plumage on the breast. Subspecies differ in their coloration and markings. None can be visually sexed.

BREED BOX	
Length	23 cm (9 in)
Incubation period	27 days
Fledging period	56 days
Clutch size	2 eggs

GOLDIE'S LORIKEETS

Goldie's lorikeet (*T. goldie*) originates from New Guinea and averages just 17.5 cm (7 in) long. They tend to be quieter than most lorikeets, and are usually quite hardy once properly acclimatized. Sexing on the basis of their head coloration or streaking on their bodies is unlikely to be reliable. The hen lays two eggs which hatch after about 24 days. The young fledge at around two months of age.

BREED BOX

Length	17.5 cm (7 in)
Incubation period	24 days
Fledging period	60 days
Clutch size	2 eggs

♦ ABOVE
Goldie's lorikeet is a very attractive species. Pairs are generally keen to breed. The calls of these birds are not loud.

MUSSCHENBROEK'S LORIKEETS

Musschenbroek's lorikeet (*Neopsittacus musschenbroekii*), from New Guinea, needs more seed in its diet than other nectar-feeding parrots, although the mixture of dissolved sugars and other ingredients is still important.

♦ RIGHT
Musschenbroek's lorikeet can suffer from tapeworms, and it may be worthwhile to have their droppings screened. Cock birds can be distinguished from hens by the more extensive brown feathering on the head.

BREED BOX

Length	23 cm (9 in)
Incubation period	26 days
Fledging period	65 days
Clutch size	2 eggs

CHATTERING LORIES

The beautiful chattering lory (*Lorius garrulus*), with the striking red plumage, is from the Moluccan Islands of Indonesia. The yellow-backed chattering lory (*L. garrulus flavopalliatus*) is instantly recognizable by the area of yellow plumage across the top of the wings. These are noisy birds, as their name suggests.

Pairs breed reliably over many years. The hen incubates the two eggs for about 26 days, and the chicks leave the nest by about 11 weeks old.

BREED BOX

Length	30 cm (12 in)
Incubation period	26 days
Fledging period	77 days
Clutch size	2 eggs

♦ LEFT
Chattering lories are robust and long-lived. Pairs are usually keen to breed. They can be noisy. Note the absence of yellow plumage across the back in this individual.

CARDINAL LORIES

BREED BOX

Length	30 cm (12 in)
Incubation period	24 days
Fledging period	70 days
Clutch size	2 eggs

Another lory with predominantly red plumage, the cardinal lory (*Chalcopsitta cardinalis*) originates from the Solomon Islands and is so named because its colour matches a cardinal's robes. It is a relative newcomer on the avicultural scene.

Pairs nest quite readily. The hen lays two eggs which hatch after 24 days. The young fledge at 10 weeks and they can be identified easily at this time by their brownish bills.

Like other members of this particular genus, such as the yellow-streaked lory (*C. sintillata*), the calls of these birds are relatively loud.

◆ R I G H T
Red plumage predominates in the case of the cardinal lory. Visual sexing, as with many lories and lorikeets, is impossible.

BLACK-WINGED LORIES

The black-winged lory (*Eos cyanogenia*) is a member of the *Eos* group of lories, which are well represented in aviculture. The red plumage is broken by areas of black or dark blue. Measuring approximately 28 cm (11 in) in length, the black-winged lory occurs on islands around the Geelvink Bay area of New Guinea. It may have a musky odour, more noticeable if the birds are housed in an indoor flight. This smell is quite normal.

BREED BOX

Length	28 cm (11 in)
Incubation period	24 days
Fledging period	77 days
Clutch size	2 eggs

◆ L E F T
The black-winged lory is characterized by the large areas of solid black plumage on the wings, although the precise extent of these areas varies between individuals.

STELLA'S LORIKEETS

The main difference between lories and lorikeets is the shape and size of the tail feathers; lorikeets' tails are longer and more tapering than lories' tails. Stella's lorikeet (*Charmosyna papou*), originating from the highlands of central New Guinea, is a striking example. Stella's lorikeets have two distinct colour phases. In the black phase, known as the melanistic form, the red feathering is largely replaced by black; in the red phase, the hen has yellowish markings in the vicinity of

◆ R I G H T
Stella's lorikeet – this one's a male – is one of the most exquisite of all lorikeets. They tend to hop rather than walk along perches. These birds become very tame in aviary surroundings.

BREED BOX

Length	38 cm (15 in)
Incubation period	26 days
Fledging period	56 days
Clutch size	2 eggs

the rump. The red areas which are retained in the melanistic cock bird allow the sexes to be distinguished.

Bills should be bright red – pale coloration is usually a sign of liver failure or other chronic illness.

DUSKY LORIES

The dusky lory (*Pseudeos fuscata*) from New Guinea has distinct colour phases. The markings of these birds are individual, varying from a fiery shade of orange to a relatively dull yellow. It can be possible to distinguish pairs by the colour of the feathers on the rump; the cock bird's are more yellow than the hen's. Pairs usually nest readily and the hen lays two eggs which hatch after 24 days. The young emerge from the nest box 10 weeks later. Like most of the larger lories, the dusky is quite hardy once properly acclimatized, especially when provided with a nest box for roosting. Chicks which have been plucked in the nest will be vulnerable to chills.

BREED BOX

Length	25 cm (10 in)
Incubation period	24 days
Fledging period	70 days
Clutch size	2–4 eggs

◆ RIGHT
This is an example of the yellow phase of the dusky lory. The coloration in this case is not as intense as in orange phase birds.

SWIFT PARAKEETS

The distinction between lorikeets and parakeets is blurred in the case of the swift parakeet (*Lathamus discolor*), also known as a lorikeet. Its tongue is not so well adapted as lorikeets' with the tiny papillae that can be raised to act as brushes to collect pollen. Seed should feature in the swift parakeet's diet, as well as fruit, greenstuff and livefood such as mealworms.

Visual sexing is difficult, though hens are generally duller in colour than cock birds. It is usually suggested that cocks have slightly larger areas of red plumage with odd red feathers evident, especially on the breast and abdomen, whereas hens are more yellow-green overall, with paler legs. Young swift parakeets are less colourful than adults, with darker irises. A yellow mutation has been recorded in the case of this species, but it is very rare. The typical green plumage is replaced by yellow in this case, with the remainder of the coloration being unaffected. It is possible to house these attractive parakeets on a colony basis in a large aviary, and they can be bred successfully in these surroundings. Introduce the pairs at the same time and provide a choice of nesting sites.

BREED BOX

Length	25 cm (10 in)
Incubation period	18 days
Fledging period	42 days
Clutch size	4–5 eggs

◆ LEFT
The swift parakeet shares characteristics with both lorikeets and parakeets. It is a southern bird, breeding on the Australian island of Tasmania and migrating back across the Bass Strait, which divides Tasmania from the mainland, for the winter.

PARROTS

Although the number of parrots favoured as household pets on the basis
of their powers of mimicry is relatively small, a much wider range of species is bred
in aviary surroundings. While some are highly destructive by nature and have loud
calls, which means that they may be unsuitable for aviaries in urban areas, there are
actually many others, such as the parrotlets, which can be housed
without great expense in a typical suburban garden aviary. The hanging parrots
can even be accommodated in a planted flight with softbills, while the colour
varieties that have been developed in the case of the peach-faced lovebird,
mean that there is plenty of scope if you are interested in colour-breeding.
Even some of the larger parrots are not especially noisy, as with members
of the *Poicephalus* group, such as the Senegal.

◆ OPPOSITE

Yellow-faced parrotlets are one of the
relatively few South American parrots
which can be sexed by sight. They are also
quiet, making them suitable for housing
in town aviaries.

◆ ABOVE LEFT

Yellow-collared macaw. Like a number of
other parrots, these particular birds have a
beautiful, almost iridescent sheen on their
green plumage, which is seen at its best in
bright sunlight.

HANGING PARROTS

There are 13 different species of hanging parrot, and distribution ranges from south-east Asia across the islands to the south. Apart from those species mentioned here, the remaining species are scarce in aviculture worldwide. Hanging parrots are small birds, about 13 cm (5 in) in length, predominantly green in colour. This allows them to blend in with their background, making them hard for predators to spot. Head markings help to distinguish one species from another.

Hanging parrots are quiet, secretive birds, preferring a well-planted flight where they can conceal themselves among the vegetation. They are not destructive or aggressive and may be kept as part of a mixed collection, including softbills. Their dietary needs are similar to softbills' – a fresh daily supply of a nectar solution and fruit such as diced apple and grapes sprinkled with a soft

food. Some hanging parrots will also eat invertebrates, such as mealworms, and many enjoy bite-size pieces of sponge cake soaked in nectar: offer the cake in a small container which is too small for the bird to bathe in, otherwise it will jump right in and its plumage will become very sticky. It is important to give these small parrots an opportunity to bathe each day. Provide a container of water for this purpose, in addition to fresh drinking water.

As the breeding season approaches, the hen cuts down leaves for nesting material, tucking these in among the feathers of her rump and transporting them back to the nest box. The nest box should be about 15 cm (6 in) square and 20 cm (8 in) in depth internally. The hen lays three eggs and these hatch after 20 days. The young emerge about a month later.

BLUE-CROWNED HANGING PARROTS

The blue-crowned hanging parrot (*Loriculus galgulus*) is probably the most widely kept member of the group. Its natural distribution extends from the Malay Peninsula southwards to Sumatra and neighbouring islands. Cocks are instantly recognizable by the circular blue area on the top of their heads and their scarlet throats. Their rumps are red, with an adjoining area of tawny yellow feathering. Hens

are much duller in comparison. They normally lack the red area seen on the throat of the cock bird, as well as the yellow band across the lower back. The highly characteristic

◆ LEFT
This blue-crowned hanging parrot is a cock bird. Interestingly, hens have occasionally been recorded as having a red throat spot, so do not rely entirely on this feature for sexing purposes.

BREED BOX	
Length	13 cm (5 in)
Incubation period	20 days
Fledging period	33 days
Clutch size	3 eggs

blue spot on the cock's crown is barely visible either. Chicks in this case are duller in plumage than hens. Their foreheads are a grey colour, with a bluish tinge, and the red feathering on the rump is much duller than in the adults. The chicks' legs are significantly paler in colour than those of the parents, and the bill is a pale horn colour, rather than black. On fledging, the young parrots are fed by the cock bird for several weeks until they are fully independent, by which stage, the hen may already have begun to nest again.

VERNAL HANGING PARROTS

The vernal hanging parrot (*L. vernalis*) occurs mainly in Asia, ranging from India to Vietnam, although it is also to be found on the Andaman Islands. Both male and female are the colour of new leaves. Cock birds may be distinguished by their white irises; the hens' irises are brown.

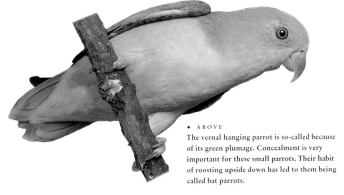

♦ ABOVE
The vernal hanging parrot is so-called because of its green plumage. Concealment is very important for these small parrots. Their habit of roosting upside down has led to them being called bat parrots.

BREED BOX

Length	13 cm (5 in)
Incubation period	20 days
Fledging period	33 days
Clutch size	3 eggs

They roost by hanging upside down off a secure perch or the aviary mesh. The roof of the flight must be covered to prevent them from being attacked by passing cats or foxes. It is important to check their claws regularly; overgrown claws hamper the bird's ability to roost.

CELEBES OR RED-CROWNED HANGING PARROTS

The attractive Celebes or red-crowned hanging parrot (*L. stigmatus*) has become more popular in aviculture in recent years. These birds are slightly larger and more active than the vernal, but they roost in a similar way, and their care is identical in all respects. They can be sexed easily.

♦ LEFT AND RIGHT
In a pair of Celebes hanging parrots, the cock bird is more colourful than the hen. These birds are not as common in aviculture as previous species mentioned.

BREED BOX

Length	15 cm (6 in)
Incubation period	20 days
Fledging period	33 days
Clutch size	3 eggs

LOVEBIRDS

This group of nine different species of small, short-tailed parrots from Africa is one of the most popular among bird-keepers across the world.

In most cases, it is not possible to sex the birds by sight and for many years breeders were forced to rely on the pelvic bone test to distinguish pairs. This method is only reliable during the breeding season, however, when the space between the hen's pelvic bones enlarges to allow for the passage of the eggs. Keeping unsexed birds on a colony basis is fraught with danger because they may fight viciously. Reliable scientific sexing methods have removed the guesswork from identifying pairs, and even though these tests can be costly compared with the price of the birds, they should ensure breeding success.

Lovebirds are generally hardy by nature, particularly when established in their quarters, but the peach-faced is especially susceptible to frostbite. These birds should not be encouraged to remain on perches in the open part of the flight when the temperature is set to drop below freezing. Most pairs will use a nest box for roosting; alternatively, design the shelter so that they can be shut in when the weather is at its worst.

The aggressive nature of lovebirds means that when they are housed in adjacent flights, the adjoining faces must be double-wired so as to prevent the birds from biting their neighbours' toes severely when they are within reach. Check the double-wiring regularly – over time, and after much aggressive biting, the mesh may sag on the frames, making contact between the birds possible. The two layers of mesh can be pushed apart again by inserting wooden notches in-between the opposite strands of mesh, to keep the two faces apart.

Otherwise, feeding and caring for lovebirds is straightforward. They will eat a diet of budgerigar seed, groats, sunflower and safflower seeds, augmented by greenstuff which must be given regularly. Soft food may be eaten when there are chicks in the nest. Lovebirds' bills are quite strong; they can whittle away branches, so be prepared to replace perches. Young hand-reared lovebirds, or those which have just become independent, can develop into friendly pets and can be taught to talk and whistle quite successfully, although they are not as talented in this respect as budgerigars. The average lifespan is 10 to 15 years.

PEACH-FACED LOVEBIRDS

The peach-faced lovebird (*Agapornis roseicollis*) is probably the most widely kept of the group, and is bred in a range of colour varieties. As the name suggests, these parrots have salmon-pink facial plumage, which is offset

♦ RIGHT
The slight green tinge on the wings of this white-faced cobalt reveals that it is not a true blue, but a dark factor form of the pastel blue.

against a green body and blue rump. They are one of the larger lovebird species at about 15 cm (6 in) in length.

The first colour mutation in the peach-faced was reported in 1954 from Japan. It is a yellow variant which retains its pink face, and is known as the golden cherry. More spectacular is the lutino, an American mutation from the 1970s. It can be identified by its red eyes and white rump.

Pied versions of the peach-faced lovebird occurred in the United States, with a separate strain being developed in South Africa. These birds were originally green with variable areas of yellow feathering. Now the pied characteristic has been combined with blue series peach-faced birds.

♦ ABOVE
The American golden cherry is in effect the yellow form of the peach-faced, with the United States mutation emerging after this colour was originally reported from Japan. It is the oldest of the peach-faced colours.

◆ LEFT
This normal pied shows roughly equal areas of yellow and green plumage. The precise markings can differ quite widely in the case of pieds.

BREED BOX

Length	15 cm (6 in)
Incubation period	23 days
Fledging period	42 days
Clutch size	4–5 eggs

The first blue variant to be developed appeared in 1963 and was of Dutch origin. Today, this variant is most commonly known as the pastel blue. These birds are not pure blue in colour, but retain a green hue to their plumage. Their facial colour is a very attractive pale salmon pink.

The appearance of a dark factor mutation, matching the dark factor seen in the budgerigar, meant that both green and blue series lovebirds could be bred in light or dark tones. The lighter coloured variants are known as dark green or jade, and cobalt, whereas those with darker coloration are described as olive and mauve. Among other peach-faced mutations which parallel those in the budgerigar are cinnamon and grey.

By combining the primary mutations, a much wider range of colour varieties has been developed, including the appropriately named buttermilk, which is a creamy pale yellow shade. There have also been changes to the facial coloration in more recent times, thanks to the creation of the orange-faced mutation, although this is still quite rare.

Not surprisingly, with such a large number of colours available, there is increasing interest in exhibiting lovebirds. The birds are very often exhibited in pairs and their appearance together can be quite stunning; a well-matched pair is certain to win over an individual if the birds are equal in other respects. Condition is vital, however, and both birds must be in perfect feather.

◆ ABOVE
The peach-faced lovebird cannot be sexed visually, but in spite of this handicap, these lovebirds are now the most widely kept of the entire group.

◆ LEFT
The orange-faced mutation affects only the facial coloration, as its name suggests. Here it is seen in combination with the dark factor jade (or dark green) mutation.

◆ RIGHT
An attractive young pair of pastel blue pieds show the characteristic but variable sea-green and pale lemon markings.

MASKED LOVEBIRDS

The masked lovebird (*A. personata*) has several colour variants, and although there are not as many as the peach-faced, it does have a much longer history.

The blue is the best-known form, in which the usual yellow areas are replaced by white, and the green by blue. There is also a dilute form of the masked, sometimes rather misleadingly called the yellow, in which the colour is paler than normal. When combined with the blue mutation, this gives rise to the so-called white, in which the blue plumage is paler and the black area on the head is much paler than normal.

The masked lovebird is a member of the white eye-ring group of lovebirds, distinguished by the prominent bare area of skin around the eyes. The group is also linked by its nesting behaviour. Nesting materials are carried to the site in the bills, rather than tucked between the feathers like the peach-faced lovebirds.

◆ ABOVE
The masked lovebird is recognizable by the black coloration, extending over its head like a mask, as well as by yellow feathering beneath.

◆ LEFT
The blue mutation of the masked has been bred for over 70 years, making it the oldest of all the known colour varieties in the lovebird group.

BREED BOX

Length	14 cm (5¹/₂ in)
Incubation period	23 days
Fledging period	42 days
Clutch size	4–5 eggs

FISCHER'S LOVEBIRDS

The widely kept Fischer's lovebird (*A. fischeri*), one of the white eye-ring group, originates from Tanzania. Fischer's construct an untidy, often domed nest in the nest box. Colour mutations exist, but are less common than in the masked. A blue form was bred in South Africa but was not established. Today's Blue Fischer's are descended from a bloodline developed in California in 1979, while in Australia a black-eyed yellow variant has also emerged.

BREED BOX

Length	14 cm (5¹/₂ in)
Incubation period	23 days
Fledging period	42 days
Clutch size	4–5 eggs

✦ LEFT
The prominent area of white skin around the eyes of Fischer's lovebird marks these birds out as belonging to the white eye-ring group. They cannot be visually sexed.

ABYSSINIAN LOVEBIRDS

The Abyssinian lovebird (*A. taranta*) originates further north than members of the white eye-ring group and, unlike them and the peach-faced, it can be sexed easily – cock birds have a broad area of red plumage extending back up the face from the bill over the eyes. Abyssinians do not construct an elaborate lining in their nest box. The hen will lay on a soft pad of feathers that may have been plucked from her own upper breast. The plumage will soon regrow.

This particular species is also known as the black-winged lovebird, thanks to the colour of its black flight feathers and the underwing coverts.

✦ BELOW
A pair of Abyssinian lovebirds in which the cock can be distinguished by the red feathering on the head. They are sometimes called black-winged lovebirds because of the colour of their flight feathers.

BREED BOX

Length	16 cm (6¹/₄ in)
Incubation period	23 days
Fledging period	45 days
Clutch size	3–4 eggs

GREY PARROTS AND ECLECTUS PARROTS

Both these species are widely bred – the grey parrot is very popular as a pet – but neither has close relatives within the parrot family. They were both brought to Europe as early as the 1500s, although it was not until much later that it was realized that the cock and hen eclectus are in fact the same species, such is the striking difference in their appearance.

The grey parrot extends right across Africa, living in the equatorial region south of the Sahara. There are two recognizable forms, the timneh and the red-tailed. The timneh (*Psittacus erithacus timneh*) is found only on the western side of the continent. It can be distinguished from the red-tailed (*P .e. erithacus*) by its smaller size, darker grey coloration, lighter-coloured upper bill and maroon tail feathers. Young birds of either type can be identified by their dark irises; mature birds have whitish irises.

Sexing grey parrots visually is very difficult, although in some cases cock birds may have recognizably darker colouring on their wings.

BREED BOX	
Length	33 cm (13 in)
Incubation period	29 days
Fledging period	80 days
Clutch size	3–4 eggs

For breeding purposes, DNA sexing is recommended, although simply having a true pair offers no guarantee of success. Compatibility is an important consideration, and it is for this reason that a proven pair of grey parrots is likely to command a premium price compared with sexed pairs which have not bred together previously. Should you find that after two years or so, a pair has shown no interest in breeding, it may be worthwhile swapping the male. Success may then follow quite rapidly, with the hen already well established in her quarters.

A standard quality parrot seed mix can be used as the basis for their diet, but a complete diet is better. Greys are prone to feather-plucking, particularly in the home, and this may be linked to poor diet coupled with lack of bathing facilities. Daily spraying is necessary if the parrot is kept in the house. Greys dislike cold damp weather and in an aviary it is vital they have suitable indoor accommodation when the weather is bad. Only well-acclimatized birds should be expected to overwinter without heating.

♦ LEFT
Grey parrots develop into excellent pets and are unrivalled mimics, but they do have a shy side to their natures.

BREED BOX

Length	35 cm (14 in)
Incubation period	30 days
Fledging period	77 days
Clutch size	2 eggs

◆ LEFT
The timneh
subspecies of the
grey parrot has a
lighter coloured
upper bill, and is
slightly smaller in
size. Young birds can
be distinguished by
their dark irises.

◆ BELOW
In the case of eclectus parrots, the cock bird is
predominantly green, while the hen is mainly
red. Young birds show these different colours
as soon as they start to feather up in the nest.

It is important to obtain a grey
parrot soon after weaning if you are
seeking a pet. They are shy birds,
and it is very difficult to win the
confidence of an untamed adult bird.
Greys nest through much of the year
and are bred and hand-reared on a
large scale, so there is usually a ready
choice of chicks available in Europe
and North America.

Eclectus parrots (*Eclectus roratus*)
do not have a fixed breeding
season, but can breed through much
of the year. Hens lay two eggs in a
clutch, with incubation and fledging
details similar to those of the grey
parrot. Pairs will often produce young
of one sex only, for biological reasons
which are as yet unclear. It is vital that
eclectus parrots have a good supply of
greenstuff such as spinach, chickweed
and dandelion as part of their regular
daily diet, along with vegetables such
as corn-on-the-cob and carrot. A
vitamin and mineral supplement is
advisable if the birds are eating seed
rather than a complete food.

POICEPHALUS PARROTS

There are nine different species of poicephalus parrot, all of which are widely distributed across Africa. The colour of the birds is variable, and they range in length from 22–30 cm (9–12 in), although they are all quite stocky and short-tailed in appearance. They need to be housed in reasonably strong aviaries, constructed using 16 gauge mesh. The timber should be protected from the birds' bills, which can cause substantial damage. These parrots make attractive aviary occupants. Adult birds will probably remain shy, but hand-reared chicks can develop into friendly companions. They have a good lifespan; Senegals have been known to live for over 40 years.

SENEGAL PARROTS

The most widely kept member of the poicephalus group is the Senegal parrot (*Poicephalus senegalus*) from west Africa. It has a greyish head and a green breast and wings. The underparts vary in colour from yellowish orange to red. Visual sexing is impossible.

Senegals are not noisy; their calls consist of a series of rasping whistles rather than discordant screeches.

The hen often flares her tail in the vicinity of the nest box as the time for nesting approaches, and she spends time inside the box before actually laying. It is essential to site the nest box in a reasonably dark corner of the aviary, preferably in the shelter, as all poicephalus parrots are reluctant to nest in the open. The hen lays three or four eggs which hatch after 28 days. The young fledge when they are about nine weeks old.

◆ LEFT
This Senegal parrot (*Poicephalus senegalus versteri*) can be distinguished by its deep orange underparts. It also tends to be a darker shade of green than other forms.

BREED BOX

Length	25 cm (10 in)
Incubation period	28 days
Fledging period	63 days
Clutch size	3–4 eggs

MEYER'S PARROTS

Meyer's parrots (*P. meyeri*), found over a wide area of eastern and southern Africa, show even greater variation in appearance than the Senegal. Generally, they are brownish grey on the head and wings, with bluish green underparts. In some but not all cases, there will be a yellow area of plumage on the crown, while all of them display yellow at the bend of the wings, at the top of the legs and on the undertail coverts. It is often assumed that slight differences in plumage provide a means of distinguishing cocks from hens but this is not the case.

Breeding details are the same as for the Senegal. Fledgling Meyer's parrots are predominantly grey with no yellow markings, and their irises are dark.

BREED BOX	
Length	23 cm (9 in)
Incubation period	28 days
Fledging period	60 days
Clutch size	3–4 eggs

♦ RIGHT
Meyer's parrot occurs in a number of different colorations, some of which are more colourful than others. These parrots cannot be sexed visually.

RUPPELL'S PARROTS

Ruppell's parrot (*P. rueppellii*), from south-west Africa, is not widely kept. Visual sexing is straightforward; unusually, the cock bird is less colourful than his mate, being silvery brown on the head and underparts, with a distinct shade of grey over the wings. Yellow markings are evident at the highest point on the wings and on the thighs. Hens have a blue abdomen, upper back and rump.

BREED BOX	
Length	23 cm (9 in)
Incubation period	28 days
Fledging period	68 days
Clutch size	3–4 eggs

Ruppell's prefer to nest during the northern hemisphere's winter months, when the likelihood of success is significantly reduced unless they are housed in indoor accommodation with extra heating and lighting available. A flight, forming part of a birdroom, is probably the best option, with the nest box indoors. Some pairs of Senegals may show a tendency to breed at this time of year, but this is less common. Ruppell's parrots may take insects when rearing their young, so mealworms should be offered to them at this stage. Other rearing foods, such as egg food, may also be eaten.

♦ LEFT
Ruppell's parrots can also be sexed by sight; the hen is the more colourful.

RED-BELLIED PARROTS

Probably the most colourful and certainly one of the most attractive of the poicephalus parrots is the red-bellied (*P. rufiventris*) from East Africa. Visual sexing is relatively straightforward; the head and wings of both sexes are brown, but the underparts of the hen are lime green and the underparts of the cock bird are brilliant orange. The cock also has green feathering on the legs.

BREED BOX

Length	23 cm (9 in)
Incubation period	28 days
Fledging period	84 days
Clutch size	3 eggs

♦ BELOW
Red-belllied parrots can be easily sexed by the colour of their underparts. It is possible to sex young chicks on this basis, as they start to feather up.

Feeding can present problems. Some birds will eat only a mixture of sunflower seed and peanuts, which are frequently a particular favourite of this group of parrots. This leaves them vulnerable to Vitamin A deficiency, and a vitamin and mineral supplement is essential. Offering a selection of fruit and greenstuff will show you what your birds like – pomegranates are often a favourite.

JARDINE'S PARROTS

Not all poicephalus parrots are found in fairly open countryside. The attractive Jardine's parrot (*P. gulielmi*) occurs in forested areas of central Africa. There are three types, varying mainly in the extent and depth of their orange plumage. The Masai (*P. g. massaicus*), from Kenya and Tanzania, has less orange-red plumage on its head and is a slightly paler shade of green than the most widely distributed central African type (*P. g. gulielmi*), which extends as far south as Angola. The northern type (*P. g. fantiensis*), from Ghana and the Ivory Coast, has paler orange markings than the others, and more prominent green edging to the feathers over the back. It is important not to pair these different types haphazardly in order to maintain the variations.

Jardine's parrots are among the larger members of the poicephalus group, averaging about 28 cm (11 in) long. Cocks have reddish-brown eyes whereas hens' eyes are brown, but this is not a reliable means of distinguishing between the sexes. The skin around the eyes is especially pronounced. However, it should not be swollen because this could indicate an upper respiratory tract infection, especially if one or both nostrils appear blocked as well.

◆ LEFT
Another Jardine's parrot reveals the difference in types. This is *Poicephalus gulielmi massaicus* from east Africa.

◆ LEFT
This Jardine's parrot (*Poicephalus gulielmi fantiensis*) comes from Liberia, the Ivory Coast and Ghana in West Africa. The orange plumage is prominent on the head in this individual.

BREED BOX

Length	28 cm (11 in)
Incubation period	27 days
Fledging period	80 days
Clutch size	3–4 eggs

PARROTLETS

As their name suggests, parrotlets are miniature parrots. There are seven recognized species of these birds, and they are all predominantly green in colour, with short, square tails. Their original distribution extends from Mexico down into South America.

Parrotlets are ideal for back garden aviaries, but these are aggressive birds and must be kept in separate pairs. They will usually nest very well. The nest box should be about 13 cm (5 in) square and 20 cm (8 in) tall, and lined with wood shavings. Despite their small size, parrotlets cannot be bred satisfactorily in flight cages; cock birds are often aggressive in these surroundings, particularly to their own male offspring. They may inflict fatal injuries

on the male chicks prior to fledging. Parrotlets are prolific when nesting, usually proving to be double-brooded, and the adult birds will probably be keen to nest a second time after chicks are hatched.

Feeding is straightforward. Parrotlets will readily take a seed mixture comprising mixed millets, plain canary seed, groats, some sunflower, small pine nuts and a little hemp, augmented by greenstuff and fruit. Seeding grasses are a particular favourite. A supplement should be given regularly, and grit and cuttlefish bone or a calcium supplement must be provided. Parrotlets can live for around 20 years or more, and have been known to breed successfully well into their late teens.

CELESTIAL PARROTLETS

The celestial (*Forpus coelestis*), the most widely kept and bred of the parrotlets, originates from parts of Ecuador and Peru, in north-western South America. It is one of the most attractively coloured members of the group and can be easily sexed. The cock bird is silvery-green; the sides of the face are of a bright apple-green and there is blue behind the eyes and on the edges of the wings. The rump feathering is blue. Hens are recognized by a less silvery tone to their plumage and a smaller blue area on the face. These little parrots make good companions if obtained at an early age, and will even learn to say a few words, although they are not talented mimics.

♦ LEFT
The celestial is the most widely kept parrotlet. These birds can be very aggressive, however, in spite of their small size.

BREED BOX

Length	13 cm (5 in)
Incubation period	23 days
Fledging period	28 days
Clutch size	4–9 eggs

YELLOW-FACED PARROTLETS

The yellow-faced parrotlet (*F. xanthops*) is found in a very restricted area of Peru. It is closely related to the celestial but at nearly 15 cm (6 in) in length, slightly larger. Distinctive facial colouring extending down to the throat sets it apart from other species. Sexing the bird is straightforward: the feathering over the rump is of a light blue shade in the hen and a deeper shade of cobalt in the cock. The yellow-faced has bred successfully in captivity and so chicks are often available. Its care does not present any particular problems.

BREED BOX

Length	15 cm (6 in)
Incubation period	23 days
Fledging period	28 days
Clutch size	4–6 eggs

♦ ABOVE
Yellow-faced parrotlets are the most colourful members of the *Forpus* group, as well as being the largest in size.

GREEN-RUMPED PARROTLETS

Some colour mutations are available in parrotlets, particularly the Guiana or green-rumped (*F. passerinus*). Unusually, the hen is more colourful in this species than the cock, with a yellow area around the bill. Among the colours which have been reported in this species are blue, lutino and cinnamon forms. These birds are popular with bird-keepers in South America. At the present time, however, they are less well-known than elsewhere. In spite of their small size, these parrotlets are quite hardy once acclimatized. Provide the hen with a nest box for nesting purposes.

BREED BOX

Length	13 cm (5 in)
Incubation period	23 days
Fledging period	28 days
Clutch size	5–6 eggs

♦ RIGHT
In the case of the green-rumped parrotlet, the hen, with the yellow on the head, is more colourful than the cock bird.

PIONUS PARROTS

There are seven species of pionus parrot, and they are widely distributed across parts of Central and South America. Although not especially well-known in bird-keeping circles, these parrots are bred regularly in small numbers and are a much better proposition, both as pets and as aviary occupants, than their larger relatives, the Amazons. Pionus parrots (their generic and common name is the same) are quieter by nature than Amazons, and they are less temperamental once they mature. Nevertheless, if you are seeking a pet, it is vital to obtain a hand-reared youngster because adults, unused to human contact, can be very shy, even in aviary surroundings.

DUSKY PARROTS

The coloration of pionus parrots may be unusual and there can be considerable individual variation. The light plays a part; seemingly drab plumage is transformed by sunlight, with shimmering shades appearing that had previously been invisible.

♦ RIGHT
Coloration is a notable feature of pionus parrots. White, brown, pink, blue and red are all apparent in the feathers of this dusky parrot.

An example is the dusky parrot (*Pionus fuscus*). In sunlight, hues of brown, pink, blue, violet and red are all apparent, with flecks of white feathering on the head.

When purchasing pionus parrots, especially adult birds, take time to watch them in their quarters before reaching any decision. Notice if the bird is perching with sleek plumage and is alert. If not, these are signs that something could be wrong, especially if coupled with any indication of weight loss over the breastbone. Also, they can wheeze rather alarmingly when handled, and it can be difficult to determine whether this is just because they are distressed by being caught, or whether they are suffering from the chronic fungal disease, aspergillosis, of which wheezing is a symptom.

Pionus parrots will benefit from a secluded aviary, and interference should be kept to a minimum when a pair do decide to breed; otherwise, these parrots may neglect or even attack their chicks. Hens lay three or four eggs which hatch after 26 days or so. The young birds leave the nest for the first time when they are approaching 10 weeks of age.

BREED BOX

Length	24 cm (9¹/₂ in)
Incubation period	26 days
Fledging period	70 days
Clutch size	3–4 eggs

BLUE-HEADED PARROTS

The blue-headed parrot (*P. menstruus*) has the greatest range of the group, extending from Costa Rica as far south as Bolivia. It is also the most commonly encountered of the pionus parrots in bird-keeping circles. It is unmistakable, thanks to the rich deep-blue plumage covering the entire head. The ear coverts are black. The blue

BREED BOX

Length	28 cm (11 in)
Incubation period	26 days
Fledging period	70 days
Clutch size	3–5 eggs

becomes reddish where it merges with the green coloration that predominates over the rest of the body. These parrots are about 28 cm (11 in) in length; they cannot be sexed visually.

◆ ABOVE
This is a blue-headed parrot. The pinkish colour on the throat is variable in extent. The upper bill is unusually coloured – black with red areas on the sides.

BRONZE-WINGED PARROTS

The bronze-winged parrot (*P. chalcopterus*) has dark blue underparts, and isolated pinkish feathers under the throat, often extending on to the head. The bill is a pale shade of yellow. As these parrots come into breeding condition, so the pink skin around their eyes darkens in colour. This area is yellow in young birds, which also have brownish feathering on their underparts.

◆ RIGHT
Like other pionus parrots, which are active by nature, the bronze-winged will benefit from having a spacious flight. Only in flight will the stunning sky-blue plumage under the wings be revealed.

BREED BOX

Length	28 cm (11 in)
Incubation period	26 days
Fledging period	70 days
Clutch size	3–4 eggs

AMAZON PARROTS

Amazons are probably the best-known group of New World parrots, having been kept as pets in Europe for over 500 years. The advent of reliable sexing methods has been partly responsible for triggering greater interest in breeding these birds, and pairs can nest reliably for many years. They also rank among the longest-living of all parrots, with an average life expectancy equivalent to our own.

Keeping an Amazon is not something to be undertaken lightly, however, because they can be very demanding birds. First and foremost, they are noisy and given to regular periods of screeching at sunrise and sunset. This is normal behaviour but is not guaranteed to endear them to neighbours who do not share your enthusiasm for these parrots.

Young Amazons can develop into excellent mimics, both of speech and sounds, although they are probably not as talented in this respect as the grey parrot. Amazons have bolder, brasher, more confident natures, however, and this is why they often do well in talking bird competitions, where they delight in running through their repertoire in front of an appreciative judging audience. There is considerable debate amongst *aficionados* about which species of Amazon has the potential to be the best mimic, but this probably depends more on the teacher than the bird.

Diet is critical to Amazons' well-being. Many species are prone to weight gain unless their diet is carefully controlled. They need a regular daily supply of roughage, vegetables and fruit, as well as seed, if they are to remain in good health, particularly as they are prone to vitamin A deficiency. Hand-reared birds often take to a complete diet, avoiding concerns over vitamin and mineral deficiencies, but it is more difficult to wean adult birds off a seed mix comprising sunflower seed and peanuts. Supplementation will be essential in this case.

Aside from becoming more vocal and destructive as the time for breeding approaches, cock Amazons may become aggressive, and if so they will not hesitate to attack you if you venture too close to the nesting site. This is a particular problem encountered with hand-reared birds because they have little if any instinctive fear of people. Careful siting of the nest box can avoid possible conflicts at this stage, allowing you to attend safely to the birds' daily requirements.

Most pairs breed in the spring. Hens lay three or four eggs in May in northern temperate areas. Incubation lasts 26–29 days. The young leave the nest seven to nine weeks later. Soaked seed is valuable as a rearing food. It will be several years before the young birds nest for the first time.

BLUE-FRONTED AMAZON PARROTS

The blue-fronted Amazon (*Amazona aestiva*), from south-eastern South America, is often kept as a pet. Young birds are recognizable by their duller coloration and dark irises. The species is one of the longest-living, and records show that individual birds have lived for almost 100 years. There is no way of sexing these birds by differences in coloration – DNA sexing will be required. Pairs should be allowed to settle in their quarters before being expected to breed. This can take a year or two, but after this they are likely to breed annually.

♦ RIGHT
In common with other Amazons, blue-fronts show variable coloration on their heads, allowing individuals to be recognized without difficulty. Some have more blue feathering above the cere than others.

BREED BOX

Length	38 cm (15 in)
Incubation period	27 days
Fledging period	60 days
Clutch size	3–5 eggs

ORANGE-WINGED AMAZON PARROTS

The orange-winged Amazon (*A. amazonica*), from north-eastern South America, is slightly smaller than the blue-fronted, averaging about 33 cm (13 in) overall. It may have some blue plumage on the head, mixed with yellow, but can be distinguished by the colour of its upper bill, which is mainly horn-coloured rather than black. The orange, rather than red, coloration on the wings and tail are further points of distinction, which separate it from the blue-fronted Amazon.

BREED BOX

Length	33 cm (13 in)
Incubation period	26 days
Fledging period	60 days
Clutch size	3–4 eggs

◆ RIGHT
Orange-winged Amazons are so-called because of the areas of orange plumage in their wings, which can be clearly seen when these parrots are in flight.

YELLOW-FRONTED AMAZON PARROTS

The yellow-fronted Amazon (*A. ochrocephala*) occurs in nine different forms throughout its wide range. These include the double yellow-head (*A. o. oratrix*), which is the variety most in demand. It is also the largest, averaging 38 cm (15 in). The head of the adult birds is entirely yellow; youngsters have yellow plumage just on the forehead and crown. Red plumage is visible on the shoulders.

In the case of the yellow-naped Amazon (*A. o. auropalliata*), which is also found in Central America, the yellow plumage is restricted to the nape of the neck, and young birds show virtually no trace of yellow on their heads.

More limited distribution of yellow plumage is a feature of the yellow-fronted Amazon itself, found in northern South America. Its bill is horn-coloured at the sides. The entire bill of the Panamanian yellow-front (*A. o. panamensis*) is a pale horn shade. This bird is approximately 30 cm (12 in) long, and is the smallest of the group.

BREED BOX

Length	38 cm (15 in)
Incubation period	26 days
Fledging period	60 days
Clutch size	3–5 eggs

◆ RIGHT
There are nine different forms of the yellow-fronted Amazon. They differ in size and in the distribution of the yellow plumage on the head.

MEALY AMAZON PARROTS

The mealy Amazon (*A. farinosa*) spans both Central and South America, the more colourful variety being found to the north of its range. The top of the head of the blue-crowned mealy (*A. f. guatemalae*) is blue, becoming greyer over the nape extending down to the mantle. Its range extends from Mexico to Honduras, and it has become better known to bird-keepers in recent years.

The mealy is the largest of the mainland species, slightly larger than the double yellow-headed Amazon. Confusion can arise between them because some mealy Amazons from South America have a yellow area on their heads, but this does not usually extend up from the cere, as it does in the yellow-fronted Amazon.

♦ RIGHT
The mealy Amazon has a voice to match its size, often proving to be the noisiest member of a raucous group.

BREED BOX	
Length	38 cm (15 in)
Incubation period	26 days
Fledging period	60 days
Clutch size	3–4 eggs

As with the majority of Amazons, visual sexing is not possible, and pairs can only be recognized with any certainty by DNA sexing. A stout aviary will be needed to house these noisy birds. Unless you have no close neighbours, the mealy Amazon is not likely to be a good choice of pet because of its loud calls. As with other Amazons, the mealy is at risk from a deficiency of Vitamin A if fed mainly on seed. Fruit and greenstuff should therefore figure in the diet, along with a vitamin and mineral supplement if the parrot is not being fed on a complete food.

WHITE-FRONTED AMAZON PARROTS

The white-fronted (*A. albifrons*), the smallest of the Amazons measuring about 25 cm (10 in) in length, is widely distributed through Central America, from Mexico southwards to Costa Rica. It is the only one of the Amazons that can be sexed on the basis of its coloration. The leading edge of the wings has red plumage in cock birds, green in hens. These Amazons may be easier to manage than their larger relatives, but they can still be noisy and they need a robust aviary with a ready supply of perches, because these will be whittled away quite frequently by the birds' powerful bills. Young white-fronted Amazons can be recognized quite easily because the area of white plumage on the head is reduced in extent and has a yellowish tinge. The red feathering around the eye is also reduced in extent. It is possible to sex these parrots by the time they fledge, thanks to the red plumage present on the wings of the males.

BREED BOX

Length	25 cm (10 in)
Incubation period	26 days
Fledging period	60 days
Clutch size	3–4 eggs

◆ LEFT
The white-fronted Amazon is instantly recognizable by the white area above the cere and the adjoining area of red plumage, which forms a narrow band around the eye. These parrots are sometimes called spectacled Amazons.

PRIMROSE-CHEEKED AMAZON PARROTS

The primrose-cheeked or red-lored Amazon (*A. autumnalis autumnalis*), from Central America, is one of the most colourful and attractive Amazons. Its black eyelashes – which are actually modified feathers – are especially evident against the white skin surrounding the eyes. Other, less colourful varieties of this species, such as Salvin's Amazon (*A. a. salvini*), occur in South America but are rarely seen in collections. Young birds in all cases have dark irises when they first leave the nest.

◆ RIGHT
In spite of its name, the primrose-cheeked Amazon manages to combine red, yellow and lilac markings on its head. It is a species which has grown in popularity over recent years.

BREED BOX

Length	33 cm (13 in)
Incubation period	26 days
Fledging period	60 days
Clutch size	3–4 eggs

MACAWS

The macaws are one of the most distinctive groups of New World parrots, thanks to the seemingly bare areas on the face which are in fact covered in patterns of tiny feathers. These thinly covered areas of skin can reflect the bird's mood, becoming redder when the bird is excited or angry.

No other group shows such a variation in size as the macaws. They range from approximately 91 cm (36 in) long down to the diminutive red-shouldered macaw (*Ara nobilis*) which is just 30 cm (12 in) in length. All macaws have a similar body shape, with long tails. The largest macaws are also the most colourful. There are no distinctive differences in plumage between the sexes, although hens can be recognized by their smaller heads.

Macaws in general are long-lived birds – they can live for well over half a century – and it may take five years or more for youngsters of the multi-coloured species to reach maturity. Youngsters can become very tame and will learn to talk, although none of the macaws is especially talented in this respect, but their powerful bills, loud voices, and for the larger ones, their size, mean that they are difficult to accommodate satisfactorily in the home environment. The dwarf macaws are easier to cater for, although they too can be noisy and are destructive by nature. In contrast to their larger relatives, they are predominantly green in colour.

It is usually not difficult to convert macaws to a complete diet compared with some other parrots. Read the instructions on the package carefully; some are only recommended for use when birds are breeding. Otherwise, walnuts, hazel and Brazil nuts should figure prominently in the diets of the larger multi-coloured macaws. Mixed nuts are obtainable from specialist seed merchants.

Macaws should be housed in individual pairs for breeding; only the red-shouldered macaw can be bred successfully on a colony basis. Stout nest boxes are essential for all macaws, in view of their destructive natures. Large reinforced barrels, mounted on secure platforms, are good for the larger species.

RED AND GOLD (SCARLET) MACAW

The red and gold macaw (*Ara macao*) has the largest distribution of any parrot in the Americas, from Mexico southwards right down to parts of eastern Peru, Bolivia and parts of Brazil. Unfortunately, however, these birds have now been declared an endangered species under the international CITES convention, largely as a result of loss of habitat in the northern end of its range. In practical terms this means that, depending on where you live, you may need to obtain official permission before you can advertise chicks that you breed for sale, or adult birds. Advice on the current situation should be obtained from the government department concerned with wildlife matters, which acts as the CITES management authority.

These particular macaws are easy to distinguish from the closely-related green-winged, not just by the golden yellow feathering over their wings, but also by their red plumage, which is scarlet rather than crimson. As a result, they are also known as scarlet macaws. It is virtually impossible to sex the birds by sight, although the heads of cock birds will often appear more bold. Young birds can be recognized by their dark irises and shorter tail feathers. The care of

◆ RIGHT
Red and gold macaws are best housed in an outdoor aviary, unless you are able to provide a purpose-built flight cage in the home.

these macaws is very similar to that of other members of the group, with nuts, seeds and fruit forming the basis of their diet, although a complete diet can also be used.

BREED BOX

Length	85 cm (34 in)
Incubation period	28 days
Fledging period	90 days
Clutch size	2–3 eggs

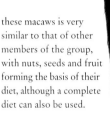

BLUE AND GOLD MACAWS

◆ BELOW LEFT
Blue and gold macaws are believed to pair for life. The members of a pair will remain close to each other, often engaging in mutual preening.

The striking blue and gold macaw (*A. ararauna*), one of the most widely kept macaws, is found over a huge area, from Panama down across much of South America. It has deep sky-blue plumage, extending from the vicinity of the crown over the entire back and wings. There is a small area of greenish plumage above the bill, and a small area of black adjoining the whitish facial skin. The tiny feather tracts on the face are unique to the individual

BREED BOX	
Length	82.5 cm (33 in)
Incubation period	28 days
Fledging period	90 days
Clutch size	2–3 eggs

bird and can be used to prove identity if a bird escapes or is stolen. Micro-chipping is a safer option, however, because there is a register to confirm the bird's identity.

An interesting mutation of this species is the blue, in which the gold is replaced by white feathering. One such bird was exhibited in France and another in the UK some years ago. In 1999, two young blue and white macaws were displayed at the UK's National Exhibition of Cage & Aviary Birds and hopes are high that this mutation can be successfully established. At present, there are no other colour variants.

GREEN-WINGED MACAWS

The green-winged (*A. chloroptera*) is another of the multi-coloured macaws, with a massive range from Panama to

BREED BOX	
Length	89 cm (35 in)
Incubation period	28 days
Fledging period	90 days
Clutch size	2–3 eggs

northern parts of Argentina. Crimson-red feathering predominates, with an area of green and blue plumage across the wings. The lower back and rump are also blue. Young birds can be identified by their dark irises and shorter tails, and by the maroon rather than crimson feathers in the prominent feather tracts extending across the face. Although gentle by nature in most cases, housing these birds in the home presents difficulties, especially as they have powerful calls.

◆ ABOVE
Like others of its kind, the green-winged macaw needs plenty of strong perches to exercise its powerful bill. Perches have to be replaced regularly as they are whittled away.

113

Yellow-collared Macaws

The yellow-collared macaw
(*A. auricollis*), well established in
aviculture, is found in Latin America,
in parts of Brazil, Paraguay, Bolivia
and Argentina. It is one of the more
colourful dwarf macaws, with a
relatively loud call. As with other
macaws, the cock and hen form a
strong bond.

BREED BOX

Length	40 cm (16 in)
Incubation period	26 days
Fledging period	70 days
Clutch size	2–3 eggs

◆ ABOVE RIGHT
The neck feathering of the yellow-
collared macaw enables it to be easily
identified. Some birds may have an
orange tinge to the yellow feathering.

◆ RIGHT
The severe macaw is one
of the less common of
the dwarf macaws in
aviculture. As with other
members of the group,
these birds cannot be
sexed visually.

Severe Macaws

The severe or chestnut-fronted macaw
(*A. severa*), less colourful than its
relatives, ranges from parts of Panama
to Bolivia and Brazil. A dwarf macaw,
it is slightly larger than the yellow-
collared. A broad band of chestnut
coloured plumage, just above the cere,
gives the bird its alternative name.
The remainder of the plumage is
predominantly green, with blue on the
head, wings and tail. Red patches are
evident on the edge of the wings, in
the vicinity of the shoulders. This
feature is seen in a number of macaws.

BREED BOX

Length	50 cm (20 in)
Incubation period	28 days
Fledging period	70 days
Clutch size	2–3 eggs

The birds often use this as a threat,
by opening their wings to reveal the
colour and intimidate a rival. They
may also use it in their mating display.

RED-BELLIED MACAWS

The red-bellied macaw (*A. manilata*) originates from northern South America. It is instantly recognizable by the maroon feathering on its lower underparts, and the bare area of pale yellowish skin on the sides of the face. While most macaws are hardy once acclimatized and easy to look after, the red-bellied has gained a reputation for being more problematic. They have a tendency to become obese very easily, which shortens their lifespan, and therefore, unless feeding a complete diet, fruit, vegetables and greenstuff should figure prominently. Offer them mixed nuts in preference to a standard parrot seed mix containing sunflower and peanuts. They will also require secluded aviary surroundings to give them a sense of security. Should the birds appear very nervous, screen the sides of the flight for added privacy until they are settled.

BREED BOX

Length	48 cm (19 in)
Incubation period	27 days
Fledging period	77 days
Clutch size	2–4 eggs

♦ RIGHT
The red-bellied macaw can be vocal, like other members of this group, and the calls of these dwarf macaws can be quite loud.

RED-SHOULDERED MACAWS

The red-shouldered or Hahn's macaw (*A. nobilis*), the smallest member of the group, is predominantly green in colour, with red markings on the undersides of the wings in the vicinity of the shoulders. They closely resemble their larger relatives and, being of a manageable size, make excellent pets. Red-shouldered macaws are more prolific than their larger relatives. Hens lay clutches of four eggs whereas bigger species may produce two or three. The incubation periods are similar, 24–26 days, but young red-shouldered macaws leave the nest at just eight weeks of age while multi-coloured macaws are likely to remain there for a further month. Just like their larger relatives, however, these so-called "mini macaws" can display their mood by blushing when excited or alarmed: the facial skin becomes redder as a result of increased blood flow.

BREED BOX

Length	30 cm (12 in)
Incubation period	25 days
Fledging period	54 days
Clutch size	3–4 eggs

♦ ABOVE
The red on the wing that gives the red-shouldered macaw its name is clearly visible in this individual.

DOVES AND PIGEONS

There are no clearly defined features that separate pigeons from doves, except that pigeons are usually larger in terms of their overall size. In fact, these names are sometimes used interchangeably in the case of some species. A number of pigeons and doves are highly coloured, with hues to rival those of parrots, but the majority will not become tame, and especially when transferred to new accommodation, they may fly around wildly and are at risk of injuring themselves. Planted aviaries are generally favoured for housing purposes, especially for the more nervous or ground-dwelling species, with the likelihood of breeding success also being increased in these surroundings. The cover helps to provide a hen with retreats where she can escape the ardour of the cock bird, as he may become very aggressive towards her during courtship. Despite their image as birds of peace, doves and pigeons can be surprisingly aggressive on occasions, and generally, pairs need to be housed individually rather than as a group. They can be kept quite satisfactorily in the company of other birds, however, although it is important to match the size of the birds carefully, as large pigeons will prove very disruptive if kept in a flight in the company of small finches.

◆ OPPOSITE
The Luzon bleeding heart is one of the
doves that inhabits areas of tropical forest,
and it will need similar cover in its aviary.
Otherwise these birds have a tendency to
become very nervous.

◆ LEFT
Names can be deceptive with this group
of birds in describing their habits. As an
example, the stocky little bare-eyed ground
dove will actually spend less time on the
ground than perched on a tree branch.

DIAMOND DOVES

Pigeons and doves may be kept as part of a mixed collection alongside finches and softbills, but they are nervous and so not suitable as household pets, with the exception of the diamond dove (*Geopelia cuneata*), which originates from Australia. These small doves, averaging about 17.5 cm (7 in) long, are quite steady by nature and can be housed in a large flight cage in the home. They may even breed in these surroundings. However, they are more usually kept in an aviary where the pairs will nest readily, laying several clutches in one season.

The diamond dove is greyish in colour, with delicate white spots over the wings. The wings are of a browner shade than the body. There is a prominent area of red skin around the eyes, which becomes more pronounced in the cock bird at the start of the breeding season.

The young are much duller than adult birds, with mottled wing markings, and the bare skin around the eyes is indistinct. It may be possible to recognize young cock birds before they moult if they start to display in the characteristic manner to hens. Courtship often takes place on the ground, with the cock bird bowing to the hen and fanning his tail feathers to her.

Pairs should be provided with a canary nest pan to support their nest, which will be constructed using pieces of moss, small twigs, feathers and other material collected around the aviary. Although these doves breed for much of the year, it is preferable to restrict breeding activity to the summer period, when success is more likely. The hen

+ ABOVE
This is the usual grey form of the diamond dove. These birds spend a lot of time on the floor of their quarters searching for seeds.

+ LEFT
The red periorbital skin surrounding the eye becomes more pronounced in cock birds at the start of the breeding period, as shown by this individual.

+ LEFT
A family of diamond doves, comprising a blue cock bird, a dilute hen and their two young chicks which have recently left the nest. Young birds are much duller in colour than adults at this stage. They are also vulnerable to chilling during prolonged spells of wet weather.

BREED BOX

Length	17.5 cm (7 in)
Incubation period	13 days
Fledging period	13 days
Clutch size	2 eggs

◆ BELOW
Red coloration in the case of these doves is of an auburn shade.

◆ ABOVE
The zebra dove is so-called because of the distinctive black and white striped patterning on its chest and underparts. These are not particularly lively birds.

◆ BELOW
The cream form of the diamond dove displays a warmer, slightly yellowish shade compared with the silver.

lays two white eggs, which hatch after 13 days. The chicks develop rapidly and fledge after a similar period of time, often leaving the nest before they are fully able to fly. This need not be a cause for concern, provided that the young doves can retreat under cover, because the cock bird in particular will continue to look after them and they will soon be perching.

Diamond doves are best accommodated as individual pairs rather than in small groups. Fighting may break out between cock birds, and breeding results are likely to be less satisfactory.

There are a growing number of colour varieties. The first was the silver; other colours include cream, fawn, chestnut-red and greyish-blue varieties. Pieds have also been developed, and wing markings with bar patterns.

Diamond doves are easy to feed. A mixture of millets is an ideal diet, augmented with other small seeds. They also eat greenstuff such as chopped chickweed. Soft food should be provided during the breeding and moulting periods.

The zebra dove (*G. striata*), slightly larger and not as widely kept as the diamond dove, occurs over a huge area from India eastwards across Asia, and down to Australia. They vary somewhat in appearance as a result of this range but, as a general guide, hens are always duller than cock birds. They require similar care.

AUSTRALIAN PIGEONS

These large birds are often to be found on the floor of the aviary, seeking out spilt seeds and other foods. During warm sunny weather, they will often sunbathe in typical pigeon fashion. This can be quite alarming at first sight, since the bird will lie at an abnormal angle, with one or both of its wings outstretched, suggesting that it may have had a fit or suffered a blow to the head. Most Australian pigeons are actually very hardy and generally long-lived, however, with pairs frequently nesting readily once they are established in their quarters.

GREEN-WINGED PIGEONS

The green-winged pigeon (*Chalcophaps indica*), also known as the emerald dove, is very colourful. Approximately 25 cm (10 in) long, its pinkish body is offset by the rich emerald-green plumage of the wings. Hens may be identified by the grey rather than whitish feathering on their foreheads.

BREED BOX

Length	25 cm (10 in)
Incubation period	13 days
Fledging period	14 days
Clutch size	2 eggs

Like many birds that originate from forested areas, the emerald dove is nervous and should be accommodated in a planted flight where there is plenty of ground cover. This will also increase the possibility of breeding success. A varied diet, including seeds, invertebrates, berries and diced fruit, along with a softbill food or pellets, keeps these doves in good condition. They can be housed in the company of non-aggressive softbills and are unlikely to interfere with them in any way because they spend much of their time on the aviary floor. Emerald doves are not hardy, even once acclimatized, and their outside flight must be well protected from the elements, with good drainage to prevent any flooding of the aviary floor.

Wicker nest baskets or a plywood platform, concealed in among the vegetation, may encourage a pair to breed. Either of these provides support for the nest, which is often a loose jumble of twigs and other material. Hens lay two eggs and incubation and rearing take about 14 days each. Remove the chicks about a week later because the adult pair may want to nest again.

◆ LEFT
This is a green-winged pigeon or emerald dove. Outside Australia, it is the Asiatic forms which are most commonly seen in aviculture. Cock birds have white or grey head markings, not evident in the Australian form.

AUSTRALIAN CRESTED PIGEONS

The Australian crested pigeon (*Ocyphaps lophotes*) is a very striking bird, not just because of its upright crest, but also on account of the kaleidoscope of colours which is the result of the iridescent plumage in the wings and tail. These pigeons are reasonably placid by nature but, nevertheless, they are better suited to an aviary where the other occupants

◆ LEFT
The Australian crested pigeon may be hard to sex, but as in the case of most pigeons and doves, established pairs will breed readily.

are of a similar size, approximately 33 cm (13 in) long, rather than being housed in the company of small birds.

Visual sexing is very difficult, although hens may be smaller than cock birds. The hen lays two eggs and the pair share incubation duties, in typical pigeon and dove style, with the cock sitting for much of the day. The young will acquire adult plumage at around six months old. Young cocks can then be recognized by their display, when the wing colours will be clearly apparent. Young birds may be nervous when first introduced to new accommodation, but they soon settle, and are quite hardy.

BREED BOX

Length	33 cm (13 in)
Incubation period	15 days
Fledging period	21 days
Clutch size	2 eggs

COMMON BRONZE WING PIGEONS

Common bronze wing pigeons (*Phaps chalcoptera*) are more nervous than Australian cresteds, but are very similar in their requirements. Hens are paler in colour than the cock birds, with greyish rather than white plumage on the head. They also lack the red coloration seen on the breast of cock birds. A pigeon seed mix, plus greenstuff and livefood, will keep

◆ RIGHT
A male common bronze-wing pigeon, showing the characteristic iridescence over the wings. Compatability can sometimes be a problem with these birds; cocks can be very aggressive at the start of the breeding period.

them in good health. Grit and cuttlefish bone should also be provided. Cocks can sometimes be aggressive towards their intended mates at the start of the breeding period, and it may be necessary to separate them briefly, taking the cock bird away from the aviary and reintroducing him later in the season.

BREED BOX

Length	35 cm (14 in)
Incubation period	16 days
Fledging period	21 days
Clutch size	2 eggs

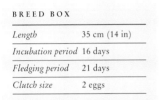

ASIATIC PIGEONS AND DOVES

A range of different species originates from Asia. It includes the various collared doves, recognizable by a black neck band, which are amongst the easiest to manage and require little more than a mixture of seed, through to the fruit pigeons and doves, widespread across the islands of south-east Asia, which need to be offered a softbill type of diet. Careful handling is necessary to avoid damaging the birds' feathers.

RED TURTLE DOVES

The attractive red turtle dove (*Streptopelia tranquebarica*) is one of the collared doves. The sexes can be easily identified because only the cock birds display the typical reddish coloration; hens are brown. These turtle doves thrive on a diet of mixed seeds and greenstuff, and can be bred successfully in mixed collections, even in the company of cockatiels. A nesting platform is important to provide support for the nest; if left to the birds to construct, the nest may

BREED BOX

Length	23 cm (9 in)
Incubation period	13 days
Fledging period	14 days
Clutch size	2 eggs

collapse, particularly if other birds attempt to steal pieces of material from it, as is highly likely.

Hens lay two eggs and incubation lasts about 13 days. The chicks grow readily and leave the nest after two weeks. In some cases, one of the chicks may be neglected, its sibling taking more of the food. Supplementary feeding at this stage, when they are feathering up, is then essential. Pairs are likely to nest several times in rapid succession, so the young should be removed as soon as they are feeding independently and transferred to another flight.

♦ LEFT
The red turtle dove – a cock bird is shown here – is also sometimes called the red collared dove. Their relatively small size and the ease of identifying pairs means that this species is a popular choice with many bird-keepers.

BLEEDING HEART DOVES

✦ BELOW
The characteristic red patch of feathering, which suggests a serious chest injury, is a feature of the bleeding heart doves. The Luzon species is shown here.

This small group of birds is under threat in many parts of their homeland, the Philippines, as a result of forest clearance. However, reasonable numbers are bred in captivity, especially the Luzon (*Gallicolumba luzonica*). As the name suggests, these birds have red plumage on their chests.

Bleeding heart doves must have a well-planted enclosure, affording them

plenty of seclusion, with heated winter-time accommodation in temperate areas. A varied diet, including livefood such as mealworms, suits them well. They spend much of their time foraging on the ground, and are likely to choose a nesting site in this area. The pair will take turns to sit, over the course of a fortnight, and the young may leave the nest at 10 days old. At this stage, they are dull brown in colour, and it will take at least six weeks for the red area on the chest to become apparent. Remove the young when they become independent.

BREED BOX	
Length	25 cm (10 in)
Incubation period	14 days
Fledging period	10 days
Clutch size	2 eggs

PIED IMPERIAL PIGEONS

Not all pigeons are adaptable in their feeding habits. The imperial pigeons, and their smaller cousins, the fruit doves, both require a softbill-type diet. They must be provided with a selection of chopped and diced fruit, sprinkled with softbill food or mynah pellets. The pied imperial (*Ducula bicolor*) is a striking example of the group, with a large gape which enables

it to swallow whole fruits such as grapes without difficulty. DNA or surgical sexing is necessary to distinguish pairs. A nesting platform should be provided. The birds use twigs, and anything else they can find as a basis for the nest. When the young pigeon first leaves the nest it will not be able to fly properly. As it starts out, it will fly around its quarters in a wild fashion, and can very easily injure itself. Take care not to frighten young birds at this early stage, to avoid provoking panic and the risk of serious injury.

BREED BOX	
Length	45 cm (18 in)
Incubation period	28 days
Fledging period	30 days
Clutch size	1 egg

✦ RIGHT
The pied imperial pigeon differs significantly in terms of its dietary needs from most pigeons and doves. It must be treated like a softbill rather than a seed-eater.

AFRICAN PIGEONS AND DOVES

Few of these species are well-known in bird-keeping circles, but their care presents no great problem. A number of species require heated winter accommodation, however, such as the Cape dove, which is often kept as part of a mixed collection alongside waxbills. Planted enclosures are recommended for wood doves in particular, greatly increasing the likelihood of breeding success with these birds.

LAUGHING DOVES

The genus *Streptopelia*, to which the turtle dove belongs, is found in Africa as well as Asia. The laughing dove (*S. senegalensis*) extends across both continents but is widely distributed across most of Africa. The plumage of the laughing dove varies within the range, but as a guide, the hens have a greyer tone on the upperparts than the cock birds. These doves grow to 25 cm (10 in) in length, and can become tame if housed in aviary surroundings.

Laughing doves require a diet of mixed seeds, including millets and canary seed. In common with other seed-eating doves and pigeons, they eat seeds whole, rather than dehusking them as finches and parrots do. Nevertheless, the doves are messy feeders, scattering seeds in search of favoured items; offer the seed mix in a food container with a broad rim to prevent unnecessary wastage.

Laughing doves are named because of their calls, although these are not loud and are unlikely to be a nuisance in terms of disturbance.

BREED BOX

Length	25 cm (10 in)
Incubation period	13 days
Fledging period	14 days
Clutch size	2 eggs

♦ BELOW
The laughing dove is a robust, popular and free-breeding species with a vast natural distribution. The African form is also known as the Senegal dove.

The birds should be provided with a nesting basket in the aviary during the breeding season. The hen will often peck at cuttlefish in her quarters before laying a clutch of two eggs. The young grow rapidly and will fledge at two weeks.

CAPE DOVES

The Cape or black-masked dove (*Oena capensis*) is a very elegant bird, reminiscent of a butterfly in flight. Only the cock bird has the characteristic black marking extending from the head down on to the chest. They are easy birds to feed, on a mixture of small cereal seeds plus some chopped greenstuff, and sometimes a small amount of livefood, but it is often difficult to persuade pairs to nest. Cape doves appreciate warm conditions, and tend to breed better in temperate areas when summers are hot. Patience is needed because, unlike many pigeons and doves, a pair may take two years or more to settle down in new

◆ ABOVE
This pair of Cape doves shows the clear sexual dimorphism that exists in this species, thanks to the black plumage of the cock bird.

BREED BOX

Length	23 cm (9 in)
Incubation period	14 days
Fledging period	14 days
Clutch size	2 eggs

quarters before attempting to nest. They will construct their nest on a canary nest pan. The chicks hatch after a fortnight, and fledge after a similar period. Cape doves are not hardy and should be brought inside for the winter, or provided with additional heat and lighting, which makes them ideal companions for waxbills. They may even prefer to breed in these conditions, so nesting facilities should be provided indoors.

WOOD DOVES

Wood doves are more of a challenge to breed than some other doves, requiring time to settle in new surroundings before attempting to nest. The blue-spotted wood dove (*Turtur afer*) is one of three species, all of which have iridescent spots on their wings. The red bill and the

◆ RIGHT
The blue-spotted wood dove uses the iridescence on its wings for display. As their name suggests, these doves benefit from being housed in a well-planted flight, which offers them a sense of security.

BREED BOX

Length	20 cm (8 in)
Incubation period	13 days
Fledging period	13 days
Clutch size	2 eggs

blue spots enable it to be distinguished from its near relatives. These wing spots form part of the cock bird's display, although they are present in the hen as well, which makes sexing difficult. While it is possible to overwinter these small doves outside in mild areas, they cannot be considered entirely hardy in temperate latitudes.

NEW WORLD PIGEONS AND DOVES

None of the doves originating from the New World are especially colourful, particularly those which are well-known in aviculture. Most have predominantly brown feathering, although it is often possible to recognize pairs without difficulty, since cocks are a brighter shade than hens. The pygmy doves are best-known, and pairs often breed well, but cocks can be aggressive towards hens in the early breeding season.

MOURNING DOVES

The mourning dove (*Zenaida macroura*) extends over a wide area of North America and the Caribbean. It averages about 30 cm (12 in) in length. Cock birds are more brightly coloured than hens and show greater iridescence on the plumage of the neck. These doves are easy to keep. Pairs breed readily but cock birds can be very aggressive

♦ LEFT
The call of the mourning dove explains how they acquired their common name.

BREED BOX

Length	30 cm (12 in)
Incubation period	14 days
Fledging period	14 days
Clutch size	2 eggs

towards their intended mate, persecuting her relentlessly and pecking at the back of her neck. It is advisable to separate them at this stage because the hen could be seriously injured or even killed by her partner. The situation usually arises because the cock is more advanced in terms of breeding condition than the hen, who does not respond to him. Try reintroducing the cock bird at a later stage; things may then proceed without problems.

House them in a planted aviary – do not expect them to nest in the open – and provide several nesting sites, giving the birds an opportunity to select a site where they feel secure. This can help to avoid conflict, especially with a pair that have not nested before. Several clutches of chicks may be reared in rapid succession, with incubation and fledging lasting approximately two weeks each. As with other doves, these birds can live for 10 years or more in aviary surroundings.

GOLD-BILLED GROUND DOVES

A number of ground doves are popular in avicultural circles, although contrary to their name, those from South America rarely spend much time on the ground. One of the best-known species is the gold-billed ground dove (*Columbina cruziana*), which is also known as a pygmy dove because of its small size. These birds average about 17.5 cm (7 in) in length, and originate from north-western South America. Cocks can be easily distinguished from hens by their more

◆ RIGHT
This is a male gold-billed ground dove. Pairs make attractive aviary occupants and often nest readily; cock birds are less aggressive towards their mates than is usually the case with similar species.

BREED BOX

Length	17.5 cm (7 in)
Incubation period	14 days
Fledging period	14 days
Clutch size	2 eggs

colourful bills and greyer heads. Hens are also duller in overall colour. A canary nest pan makes an ideal nesting receptacle for them, and these doves can be bred in the company of finches and small softbills, but they should be kept apart from their own kind because they will prove to be aggressive. Gold-billed ground doves can live for over 10 years.

BARE-EYED GROUND DOVES

While virtually all pigeons and doves nest in the open, the bare-eyed ground dove (*Metropelia ceciliae*), which originates from the Andean region of South America, is unique in requiring a nest box for breeding. They also roost in the box. These doves are quite hardy once acclimatized. Breeding behaviour is otherwise the same as that of other ground doves from the region. Chicks should be removed as soon as they become independent because the adult birds are likely to continue with a second nest.

BREED BOX

Length	15 cm (6 in)
Incubation period	14 days
Fledging period	14 days
Clutch size	2 eggs

◆ ABOVE
The bare-eyed ground dove is an unusual and often pugnacious species. Cock birds may have more reddish-brown underparts, but this is not an infallible way of sexing these doves.

INDEX

NOTES

NOTES

NOTES

NOTES